Pensacola Fortifications, 1698-1980

GUARDIANS ON THE GULF

James C. and Irene S. Coleman

A Society book commemorating the sesquicentennial of Old Christ Church, Florida's oldest standing church building, 1832-1982; and the 50th anniversary of the founding of the Pensacola Historical Society, 1933-1983.

Pensacola Historical Society 1982

 Printed by Bodree Printing Company, Inc., Pensacola, Florida.

ISBN 0-939566-02-8

The Pensacola Historical Society is a not-for-profit educational organization which operates the Pensacola Historical Museum in Old Christ Church. The Society is dedicated to the preservation of Pensacola and West Florida history and heritage through museum collections, monthly programs for its members and guests, and through publication of books and periodicals. Society programs are operated from public and private contributions with an Endowment Trust Fund for tax-deductible gifts and memorials (I.R.S. No. 59 0917279).

Front cover: Barbette guns of Fort Pickens firing on Confederate Forts McRee and Barrancas in Pensacola harbor on the morning of November 22, 1862. From *The New York Illustrated News*. Design by Adrian Enfinger and Jesse Earle Bowden.

Back cover: Lieutenant Kenneth Whiting, piloting an AB-2, made one of the first catapult shots from a barge in Pensacola Bay in 1916. Picture donated to the Pensacola Historical Museum by Vice Admiral Wendell G. Switzer.

Contents

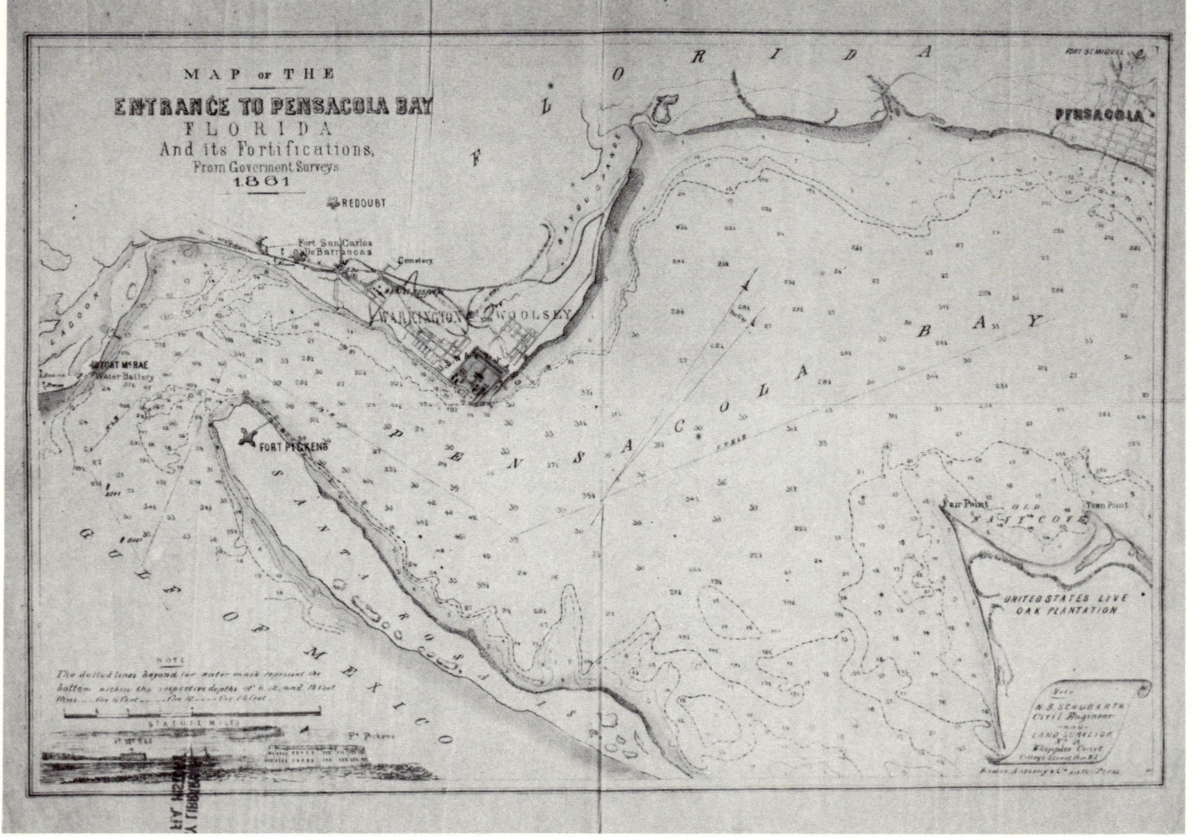

1861 U.S. Coast Survey map of Pensacola Bay and harbor fortifications. Landmarks include Fort McRee on Foster's Bank, Fort Pickens on Santa Rosa Island, Fort San Carlos de Barrancas on the mainland near the U.S. Navy Yard, and the town of Pensacola. Map courtesy of P.K. Yonge Library, University of Florida.

Introduction

For nearly 300 years the history of Pensacola has been intimately linked to its military installations. These have ranged from simple log and sand embankments to elaborate masonry forts; from small smooth-bore mortars behind a sand-bag parapet to large rifled cannon within a reinforced concrete bunker; from temporary cantonments of log huts or tents to permanent stations having all the facilities of a city.

How did this widely varied assortment of military posts, camps, stockades, airfields, and forts happen to be built in and around Pensacola? Who were the men that built them; and for what purpose? Who attacked and who defended them when war came? How many installations preceded those we see today? Where were they built? Why? What happened to them?

No United States coastal city has had a more varied history, or has had the variety of military installations than those built on the sandy shores of Pensacola Bay. The authors have compiled a record of these facilities and have described those that have played a more important part in Pensacola's history.

The span of time covered is from early in the sixteenth century to the present. However, the greatest emphasis has been given to the earlier chapters in the story of Pensacola; the centuries of sail and steam and of the early flying machines. This was also the period of fixed coastal fortifications constructed to defend a narrow band of land and water along the nation's shores. The vast installations of the present day are listed, but are not described. The story of the *Guardians on the Gulf* in the Space Age remains to be written.

Chronology of Major Pensacola Fortifications

1559	Don Tristan de Luna y Arellano established the first Spanish settlement on Pensacola Bay. The settlement was abandoned two years later. Its exact location is not known.
1698	Admiral Andres de Arriola established Fort San Carlos de Austria near present site of Fort Barrancas.
1719	Matamoros de Isla, Spanish commandant, built a small stockade, Fort Principe de Austurias at Punta de Siguenza on Santa Rosa Island, located on western tip of island near present Fort Pickens.
1719-1722	Spanish and French troops exchanged possession of Pensacola Bay four times. France retained possession until 1722.
1722	The Spanish returned. They abandoned the ruined San Carlos de Austria in favor of a new presidio on Santa Rosa Island. The new fort was called Santa Rosa Punta de Siguenza.
1750 (c)	A small fort, San Miguel, was erected on the mainland at the present site of Seville Square, downtown Pensacola.
1752	Santa Rosa de Punta de Siguenza was destroyed by a hurricane. The survivors moved to Fort Miguel on mainland.
1757	San Miguel de las Amarillas, the mainland fort, was renamed Panzacola by royal order of King Ferdinand VI.
1763	Treaty of Paris. The British occupied Pensacola and its fort. The Spanish left the Pensacola Bay area.
1771	British built a fort at the Barrancas. This fort was referred to as Red Cliffs, Upper and Lower Batteries, and finally, as the Royal Navy Redoubt. A small battery was also placed at Tartar Point.
1771-1781	The British rebuilt old Spanish fort, San Miguel, and named it Fort at Pensacola. They built Fort George, Queen's Redoubt, and Prince of Wales Redoubt on Gage Hill.
1781	The British surrendered Fort George, Queen's Redoubt, and Prince of Wales Redoubt, all in Pensacola, to the Spanish under General Galvez.

Royal Navy Redoubt at the Barrancas was also surrendered. The Spanish renamed the forts Fort San Miguel, Fort San Bernardo, Fort Sombrero, and Fort San Carlos de Barrancas.

1793 The Spanish built a battery at Punta de Siguenza.

1797-1798 The Spanish built a new fortification below the old San Carlos de Barrancas. They named this medialuna the Battery San Antonio. They rebuilt San Carlos de Barrancas.

1812 War between United States and Great Britain.

1814 Andrew Jackson arrived in Pensacola, November 6. He demanded evacuation of the British troops, given permission by the Spanish to occupy the area. Jackson attacked, and Spanish surrendered Pensacola, November 7. The British withdrew, demolishing Fort San Carlos de Barrancas, the battery on Santa Rosa Island, and spiking the guns of Battery San Antonio.

1817 New Fort San Carlos de Barrancas built by the Spanish one hundred yards east of old fort.

1818 Jackson returned to Pensacola. The Spanish commandant made his stand at Fort San Carlos de Barrancas, but surrendered it May 26.

1821 Spain ceded Florida to United States. Jackson returned to Pensacola to receive Florida from the Spanish. American flags were raised over Fort San Carlos de Barrancas and forts in town.

1825 U. S. government created the Navy Yard and made plans for the defense of the bay. The Army transferred Barrancas area to the jurisdiction of the Navy.

1829 Construction of Fort Pickens was begun. The fort was completed in 1834.

1834 Construction of Fort McRee was begun. It was completed in 1837.

1839 Battery San Antonio redesigned and repaired. Construction of Fort Barrancas was begun. The fort was completed in 1844.

1844 Army resumed control of the Barrancas area.

1845 Florida was admitted to the Union. Advanced Redoubt of Fort Barrancas was begun.

1846 Mexican War. Fort Barrancas was used as staging area; Navy Yard busy.

1851 Barrancas Barracks occupied. It was used until 1930s.

1861 **Jan. 8.** First shots of Civil War fired at Fort Barrancas.
Jan. 10. Florida seceded from the Union.
Jan. 12. U. S. Navy Yard, Fort Barrancas, and Fort McRee were surrendered to Florida militia. Union soldiers removed to Pickens.
Oct. 9. Battle of Santa Rosa Island. Confederate troops from Fort

Barrancas assaulted Federal troops at Fort Pickens.
Nov. 22 & 23. Federal guns at Fort Pickens and ships bombarded Forts McRee and Barrancas and Navy Yard.

1862 **Jan. 1 & 2.** Second artillery duel between Confederate and Union forces. **May 10.** Confederate forces evacuated Pensacola. Union troops occupied Fort Barrancas and the Navy Yard.

1865 Civil War ended.

1870s Fort Barrancas became a training station for the Coast Artillery. New buildings constructed at Post of Fort Barrancas. No further work was done on the Advanced Redoubt of Barrancas.

1886-88 Apache Indians under Geronimo worked on forts.

1895-1906 Construction of batteries Cullum, Worth, Van Swearingen, Pensacola, Center, Servier, Payne, Trueman, and Cooper on Santa Rosa Island.

1898 Spanish-American War.

1911 Navy Yard placed on caretaker status.

1914 Naval aviation training established at Pensacola.

1916 Fort Barrancas and Post of Fort Barrancas used as training areas for ROTC and national and state guard units.

1917-1923 Battery Langdon is constructed.

1921 Civilian Military Training Corps training was begun at Fort Barrancas.

1930s Regional headquarters for the Civilian Conservation Corps established at Fort Barrancas.

1941- World War II. Naval Air Station trained thousands of aviators. Auxiliary landing fields and training stations established.

1947 Fort Pickens and Fort Barrancas declared obsolete as Coast Artillery installations. Army relinquished the land at Fort Barrancas to the Naval Air Station.

1949 Fort Pickens area taken over by Florida Board of Parks.

1971 Fort Pickens acquired by National Park Service.

1972 National Park Service acquired Fort Barrancas, the Advanced Redoubt of Fort Barrancas, Battery San Antonio, and Fort Pickens as part of the Gulf Islands National Seashore. Restoration program was begun.

1976 Restored Advanced Redoubt of Fort Barrancas dedicated.

1981 Restored Fort Barrancas and Battery San Antonio (Water Battery) dedicated.

Early Spanish Forts

Name: San Carlos de Austria

Dates: 1698-1719

Location: On high ground north of Pensacola Bay, near present Fort Barrancas.

Built By: Spain.

Designed By: Jaime Franck, Austrian military engineer, serving with the Spanish expedition.

Description: Quadrilateral in shape with bastions at the corners. About one hundred yards on a side.

Materials Used: Pine stakes and logs; sand.

Armament: Initially twelve guns, 8- and 10-pounders. Heavier artillery added later. In 1718, twenty-eight guns listed.

Garrison: Original expedition had about 350 to 400 troops and laborers. Later population varied between one hundred and 300.

Present Status: Destroyed by the French in 1719. Not rebuilt by the Spanish. No remains of fort have been found.

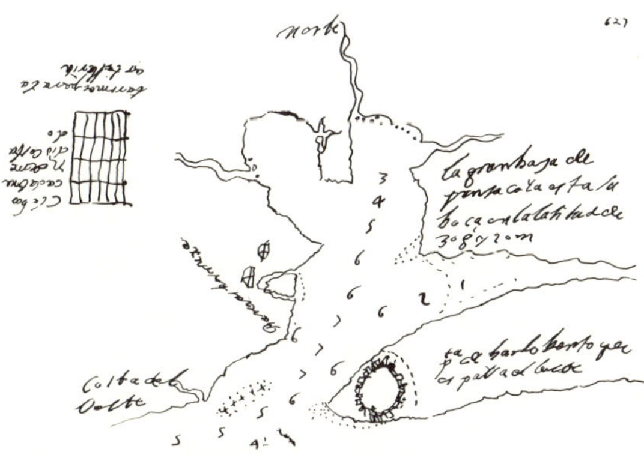

Santa Maria de Galve (Pensacola Bay) in 1698 with proposed Spanish fortifications. Sketch based on an original map by Austrian military engineer Jaime Franck in 1698. Original photo from Florida Historical Quarterly, Vol. 37, Nos. 3-4. P. 233. Reproduction by Dianne Dusevich.

Name:	Santa Rosa Punta de Siguenza
Dates:	1722-1752
Location:	Western end of Santa Rosa Island, east of Fort Pickens, near Battery Worth.
Built By:	Spain.
Designed By:	Construction under the general direction of Don Alejandro Wauchope.
Description:	Square stockade with single palisade. Presidio nearby with many buildings.
Materials Used:	Logs and sand.
Armament:	12-pounder guns.
Garrison:	Varied, but always small.
Present Status:	Allowed to deteriorate after the hurricane of 1752. Site located and excavated in 1964. No visible remains today.

Name:	Fort San Miguel
Dates:	Begun as outpost in late 1740s. In 1752 became main Spanish settlement.
Location:	Mainland; present downtown Pensacola, near Seville Square.
Built By:	Spain.
Designed By:	Governor Don Miguel Roman de Castilla y Lugo in charge of construction.
Description:	Square stockade of pointed stakes with four semi-bastions. Approximately 700 by 400 feet. Auxiliary batteries in area.
Materials Used:	Logs and sand.
Armament:	At one period, twenty-one cannon and seventeen smaller pieces listed at fort.
Garrison:	1761, about 150 men.
Present Status:	Fell into disrepair. Replaced by British Fort of Pensacola. Nothing remains today.

Early Spanish Forts

For two centuries after the discovery of America, the Gulf of Mexico was a Spanish lake. It was not until the late decades of the seventeenth century that France and England began seriously to challenge this domination. In 1693, Spain, concerned about the expeditions and explorations of these rivals, sent Don Carlos de Siguenza y Gongora to the Gulf of Mexico to investigate the Pensacola Bay area as a possible site for a new colony and fortification. His report was extremely enthusiastic about the advantages of the bay and the surrounding territory. He declared that there was no place better adapted than Point Siguenza and the Barrancas. Thus, Siguenza recognized the strategic importance of the western tip of Santa Rosa Island (Point Siguenza) and the mainland heights (the Barrancas) as defensive positions.[2]

It was not until 1698 that this recommendation was acted upon. In November of that year, an expedition, numbering between 350 and 400 men, under the command of Andres de Arriola, landed at the Barrancas and quickly established gun emplacements at the crest of the heights.[3] This was the first Spanish fortification to be built in the Pensacola area. It was named San Carlos de Austria, honoring Carlos, the son of the Austrian emperor and his wife, the Spanish king's sister, and therefore, the nephew-in-law of the reigning Spanish monarch.[4]

It had been spring when Siguenza had explored the bay region in 1693. Arriola's 1698 expedition arrived in a dreary November after a stormy passage through the Gulf, and he could find few of the advantages that Siguenza had extolled. In letters to his superiors he reported that a fort on the bluffs could not defend the entrance channel. Even a second fortification on the island at Point Siguenza would be of little help because the channel was so wide. Moreover, it would be almost impossible to build the island battery because of the unstable sand and the low elevation of the site. Neither did he think the French posed a serious threat at Pensacola.[5] Nevertheless, Arriola, though disillusioned with his assignment, followed his orders and built the Fort San Carlos de Austria on the bluffs, but nothing was constructed on Santa Rosa Island.

Jaime Franck, an Austrian military engineer with Arriola's expedition, was in charge of building the fort.[6] The fortification, about one hundred yards square, was of necessity made of wood, as no stone was available in the area. "In design and construction San Carlos was a typical field redoubt* of the period. On each side of a quadrilateral that an engineer officer traced on the crest, pine stakes some two inches thick were set deeply into the sand in two parallel rows perhaps six yards apart. Held in place by these sunken footings two rows of pine logs (each about nine yards in

* A Glossary of Technical Terms begins on page 111.

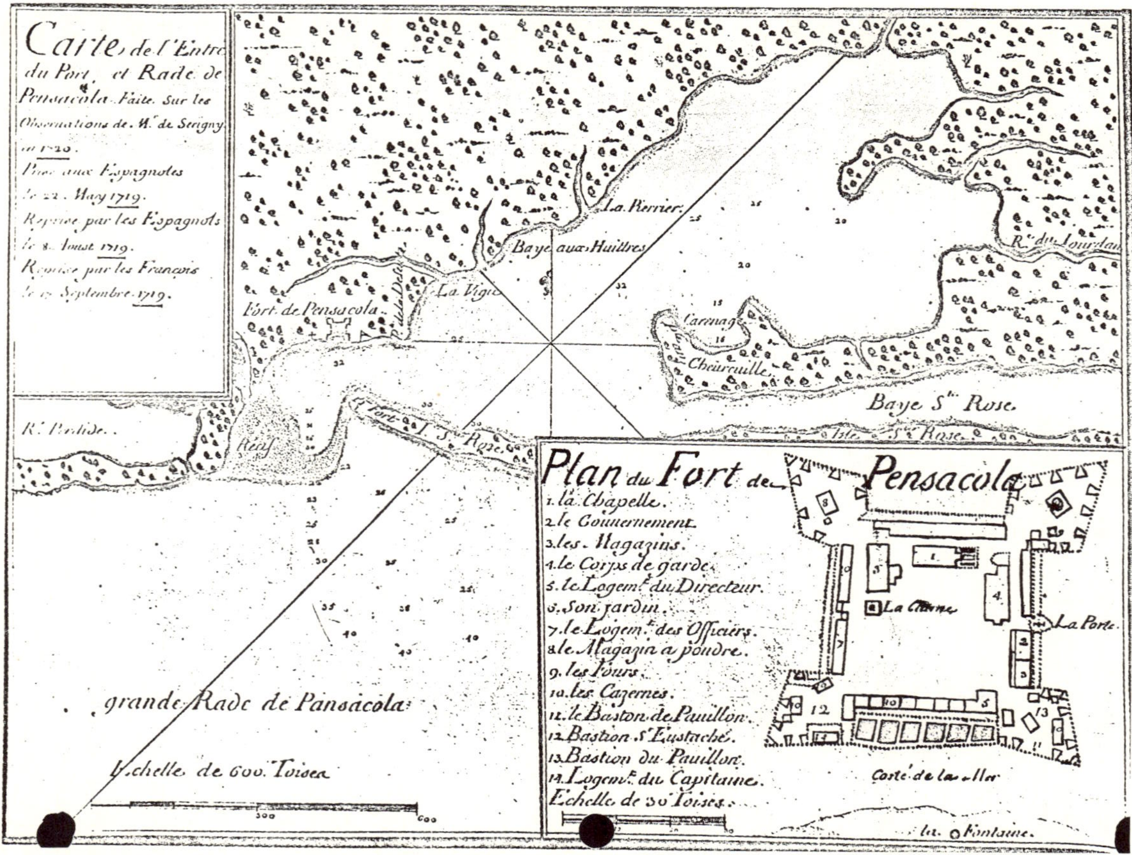

Fort San Carlos de Austria around 1719, when Spanish and French struggled for control of Pensacola Bay and Spanish Florida. A fort is shown on the western tip of Santa Rosa Island. Photo courtesy Historic Pensacola Preservation Board.

length and one foot thick at the base) leaned inward and upward and joined their tips, like the rafters of a gable, some twenty-five feet above ground. Within the space thus enclosed, triangular in section, a terreplein or earthfill of sand was shoveled and poured even to the top; sand and timbers became a fascine embankment strong enough to resist the assault of heavy guns. At each of the four angles a rhomboid bastion, almost square, projected obliquely to give the defenders vantage for artillery fire upon any enemy who should approach the foot of the curtain, or wall. During nearly one hundred years the Spaniards of Pensacola were not to improve upon this method of defense except by use of an adventitious exterior ditch, which was wanting in the case of the first San Carlos."[7]

The twelve guns brought by Arriola for San Carlos de Austria were 8-pounders and 10-pounders.[8] Later, heavier armament was added. The fort was extremely difficult to maintain in good condition. The pine logs rotted away; the sand eroded from the terreplein; storms damaged the buildings both inside and outside the fortification.[9] However, a sturdy powder magazine, lined with pine logs, was constructed under the sand, capable of withstanding both the dampness and the fires.[10] The location of the fort in an area overlooked by higher dunes made it difficult to defend from the land side, and military supplies from both Mexico and Spain were slow to arrive.[11]

Fires were a constant hazard because the huts were thatched with palmetto leaves which rapidly dried out. Franck wrote of one fire which took place in January, 1699. It began "through the carelessness of gamblers. Some soldiers' barracks, the chapel, Jordon's quarters [one of the officers] ...and the provision magazine were consumed by fire in less than a quarter hour. Nothing of mine was burned, but I was robbed a plenty." Little wonder that Franck concluded one of his letters by referring to San Carlos de Austria as a "disagreeable wilderness" and saying that he had never been "in such a sorry job."[12]

Added to these difficulties was the fact that the garrison was never at full troop strength, and the caliber of the troops left much to be desired. Many of them were criminals "whereby the jails and junk shops of Mexico... [were] cleaned out."[13] Life at the fort was hard. The men and officers lived in primitive barracks and huts, and their pay was small and erratic.[14] Auxiliary buildings, such as warehouses, a chapel, guard house and hospital, were built either within or close by the stockade. A cemetery was established to the west of the compound.[15] With so little to offer, it was difficult to recruit soldiers and laborers.

The population fluctuated between one hundred and 300 people. In 1713, 212 persons were reported at San Carlos de Austria, including twenty-five women. Civilians at the post included carpenters, blacksmith, some Indians, and, occasionally, chaplains and medico-friars. The task of provisioning these people was never adequately solved. The area itself was not fertile enough for large crops, and food staples had to come from Mexico.[16] Several times the French forts to the west sent supplies to San Carlos de Austria in order to prevent starvation.[17] Despite these conditions, Spain maintained the fort.

The first test of strength came to this lonely outpost of the Spanish Empire even before it was completed. On January 27, 1699, a fleet appeared at the entrance of the harbor. The fort and the ships in Pensacola Bay were quickly put in the best possible condition, for the visiting ships were flying the French flag. Although France and

Spain had been at war in Europe, they had recently signed a peace treaty; consequently, after an exchange of visits by the officers, the French, under Pierre Le Moyne d'Iberville, moved along the coast to the west without any hostilities having developed.[18] Jaime Franck congratulated himself for having the fronts of the fort, those facing the water, completed, so that when the "leader of the French squadron saw it, he perceived both it and our determination."[19]

Subsequent history of the fort included many fires and severe storms. In 1707, a series of Indian raids began. The garrison, weakened by short rations, poor equipment, and the usual illnesses, skirmished for several weeks.[20] When the Indians eventually withdrew, they took with them four horses that belonged to the garrison, plus clothing and other scarce items.[21] Although one commandant after another pleaded for more troops and more armament, San Carlos de Austria continued to be the step-child of both the Spanish and Mexican governments. When Matamoros de Isla became commandant in 1718, he found San Carlos de Austria without an exterior ditch or a parapet, and with nine of its twenty-eight guns useless. At that time there were only two companies of men assigned to the post.

Siguenza's original suggestion for a fortification on the western end of Santa Rosa Island to complement San Carlos de Austria in the defense of the entrance to Pensacola Bay had never been carried out. Several of the earlier Spanish commandants realized that no installations at these points could adequately control the entrance channel because the channel was too wide for the type of guns available. Matamoros de Isla, knowing that France and Spain were again at war, decided he had to fortify Point Siguenza, the western tip of Santa Rosa Island.[22]

In May 1718, Don Antonio Jose Martinez, an engineer, was sent from Vera Cruz to begin work on this new fortification and to strengthen Fort San Carlos de Austria. To supplement the few laborers available, soldiers were put to cutting stakes, but even with their help the work proceeded slowly because of hot weather and sickness. Early in 1719, Spain sent fifty-seven additional men and another engineer, Don Jose Berbegel to Pensacola Bay. Berbegel informed Matamoros that San Carlos de Austria was so deteriorated that it could not be defended. He recommended that it be abandoned in favor of the Point Siguenza fortification. Matamoros did not follow this suggestion. Instead, he divided his labor force between the mainland and the island. He built huts at Point Siguenza so that the workers could live there instead of traveling back and forth to the mainland.

The fortification built at Point Siguenza was a bastioned stockade mounting a battery of three 12-pound guns. It was garrisoned by twenty soldiers.[23] Work was scarcely completed on the fort when a small French fleet sailed into the bay and attacked Point Siguenza on May 13, 1719. The little garrison was captured. A detachment of soliders, routinely sent from San Carlos de Austria as a change of guards, was also taken prisoner.[24] Guns were spiked, and the French reassembled their troops and ships for a strike at San Carlos de Austria. Delayed at first by poor winds, the fleet was finally able, on May 17, to move into the bay, passing under the guns firing from the bluffs. On May 19 the terms of surrender were agreed upon. San Carlos de Austria and Point Siguenza were taken over by the French, and the Spaniards were allowed to go to Havana.[25]

The capture of San Carlos de Austria and Point Siguenza was the beginning of the confrontation between France and Spain in Pensacola Bay. Between 1719 and 1722 the area changed hands several times. While the French were in control they did little to maintain either the island or the mainland fort.[26] Once when the Spaniards returned, they reconstructed the battery at Point Siguenza and named it Fort Principe de Austurias.[27]* They also strengthened San Carlos de Austria, but to no avail. They could not hold the territory when the French returned for another attack. Finally, the issue was decided in Europe.

In 1722, as a condition of the treaty ending the War of the Quadruple Alliance, France reliquished its claims in Pensacola Bay, and Spain controlled Pensacola once more.[28] When the Spaniards returned, they found only one cabin, a bake oven, and a lidless cistern at San Carlos de Austria. The guns there, and on Santa Rosa Island, were all useless and covered with sand.[29]

Spanish Forts 1722-1763

The returning Spanish had orders to build a new fort, not in the old location on the Barrancas, but at a new site on Santa Rosa Island. Point Siguenza was not a suitable place for a fort of any size. The exposed low position, plus the unstable sands, were disadvantages that could not be overcome. Instead an area three quarters of a mile east of Point Siguenza and about one hundred yards from the northern shore of Santa Rosa Island was chosen. This location could still offer some defense of the channel; and it was hoped that in time a new fort on the mainland, at a location east of the old San Carlos de Austria, would be erected.[30]

Don Alejandro Wauchope was selected to command this new enterprise. He arrived in Pensacola Bay on November 25, 1722 with orders to evacuate the Spanish post on St. Joseph's Bay (east of present-day Panama City, Fla.) and to remove its occupants to Santa Rosa Island. He sent his ships to St. Joseph's to bring the sixty soldiers and Captain Pedro Primo de Rivera to the new presidio, Santa Rosa Punta de Siguenza. Along with the men, artillery and supplies of all kinds were brought. Building was begun immediately, and in February, 1723, the presidio had the following buildings:

> A warehouse forty feet long, twenty feet wide, and twenty feet high, from cedar boards, and nails from Vera Cruz; a powder box, made of the same material, fifteen feet long, ten wide, and five high, covered with hides; a paymaster office of material from Vera Cruz, twenty feet long, nine wide, and nine high; two barracks, each forty feet long, eighteen feet wide, and eight high, constructed of the same material, except for the roofs, which were brought in from San Joseph; a house for Captain Pedro Primo de Rivera, twenty feet long, ten wide, and ten high, made of boards from San Joseph, and nails from Vera Cruz; a powder magazine, ten feet long, eight wide, and eight tall, constructed of boards from San Joseph; twenty-four small buildings built also of San Joseph material, roofed with bark, for the dwellings of

* A list and short description of each of the military installations in the Pensacola area begins on page 92.

> workmen, convicts, and other persons of the populace; eight large houses for the top officers; a bake oven for bread; and a lookout of thirty-seven cubits [about fifty feet], built between two trees, with steps leading up to it."[31]

The stockade itself was a little to the east of the main settlement. It was a single square palisade, similar in construction to the earlier Spanish fort. It was built of logs and set upon a foundation of piles driven deep into the sand, and it was fortified with 12-pounder guns. This stockade was never called upon to defend the bay.

In the 1740s, Spain was still apprehensive of the French located to the west at Mobile. In 1744, Field Marshall Pedro de Rivera y Villalon was commissioned by the Spanish government to review the defenses of Pensacola Bay. At that time, there was some agitation to move the principal fortification back to the mainland. Many of the guns had become unserviceable,[32] and the garrison was depleted. Rivera noted the poor condition of the presidio, and he added in his report that "in the 45 years since the occupation of Pensacola Bay by our forces, no suitable fortification has been constructed for the defense of that territory." In spite of this conclusion, he did not recommend abandoning the bay altogether; neither did he recommend a move to the mainland.[33]

A move was finally dictated in 1752. Although the island had always been subjected to storms, the hurricane it experienced in that year was particularly severe. When the storm was over, Santa Rosa Punta de Siguenza was no longer habitable. Part of the population transferred to the mainland to the block house known familiarly as Fort San Miguel; government officials moved a quarter mile east on the island and built a blockhouse, receiving aid from the French at Mobile to do so. (The colonies of Mobile and Pensacola helped each other from time to time despite the enmity of the mother countries.) The fortification on Santa Rosa Island was located on ground slightly higher than the old presidio, and it housed eight guns. This little stockade apparently remained in use until it was surrendered to the British in 1763, along with San Miguel. It was probably in no better condition than San Miguel, but the British repaired it and used it as a signal outpost for many years.[34]

Fort San Miguel had been established on the mainland (near the Seville Square area of present-day Pensacola) in the late 1740s.[35] The "fort" was a small blockhouse with a garrison of eight soldiers and one non-commissioned officer. It had been established to protect a small Indian mission in that area. This mainland settlement became, after the 1752 hurricane, the principal Spanish installation on the bay.[36] The Viceroy in Mexico, the Marquis de las Amarillas, named the new fort after himself, calling it Fort San Miguel de las Amarillas. However, the King of Spain, by royal order, decreed that the name should be San Miguel de Panzacola.[36]

At that time, Pensacola did not have a genuine stockade. Disease had reduced the number of troops, the magazine was almost empty. News of Indian raids spurred the new governor, Don Miguel Roman de Castilla y Lugo, to begin construction of a stockade. While he awaited the completion of the fort, Roman constructed a series of batteries with swivel guns and cannons, and these he dispersed around the area. At that time he had about 150 troops in his command.

Eventually, the fort was built. It was rectangular with four demi-bastions. Within its walls were a blockhouse, church, warehouse, barracks, hospital and several other buildings.[37] Bricks designated for government buildings were used, instead, for the commandant's own house.[38] Other buildings, both inside and outside the stockade had thatched roofs — an ever-present fire hazard. The fort, when finished, was enclosed on all four sides. It measured about 700 feet east to west along the shore of the bay and about 400 feet north to south. The perimeter consisted of a single line of pointed posts, reinforced at intervals with a second line of posts with sand fill between the two. The demi-bastions housed twenty-one cannon and seventeen small pieces.[39]

When the Indians attacked in 1761, the inhabitants of the area, except for the few women who were sent to Havana, had to come into the stockade. Movement outside the palisade was limited to the distance the guns could fire. Cavalry had to escort people to the creek for water. The effective garrison was not more than 150 men, and supplies were short, as usual. Storms continued to batter the buildings. A new governor arrived in 1761, and he found the barracks without roofs and the fort in shambles. He tried as best as he could to repair the stockade, but when the British took possession in 1763, the fort was still in such poor condition that only forty-four miscellaneous pieces of artillery remained, and the holes in the palisades were so large that people could walk through them.[40]

The Spaniards left Pensacola Bay in 1763. They had controlled the area since 1698, except for the few years between 1719 and 1722 when France challenged their supremacy. The cost of this occupation has been estimated at $36,389,609 (1978 value).[41] For Spain, the dream of a Gulf Coast Empire had indeed been expensive.

The exact location of San Carlos de Austria has never been determined. It probably was in the general area of the present Fort Barrancas, but, as yet, there have been no positive finds to prove where it sat. Time and eroding sands have changed the contours of the bluffs, and it would be difficult to find any ruins of the fort. Likewise, nothing remains of the small fortifications at Point Siguenza. However, in 1964, excavations conducted by the Department of Anthropology of the Florida State University did reveal the location of Santa Rosa Punta de Siguenza as being east of Fort Pickens, near Battery Worth.

Santa Rosa de Punta de Siguenza on Santa Rosa Island, 1723-1752. Originally published in Roberts: Accounts of Florida, London, 1763, *the drawing by Dom Serres is a view from the north: Spanish fort, church, Governor's house, Commandant's house, a well, and a bungo. Sketch was the basis for the reconstructed Spanish village on Santa Rosa Island for Pensacola's Quadricentennial in 1959.* Photo/Pensacola Historical Society Collections.

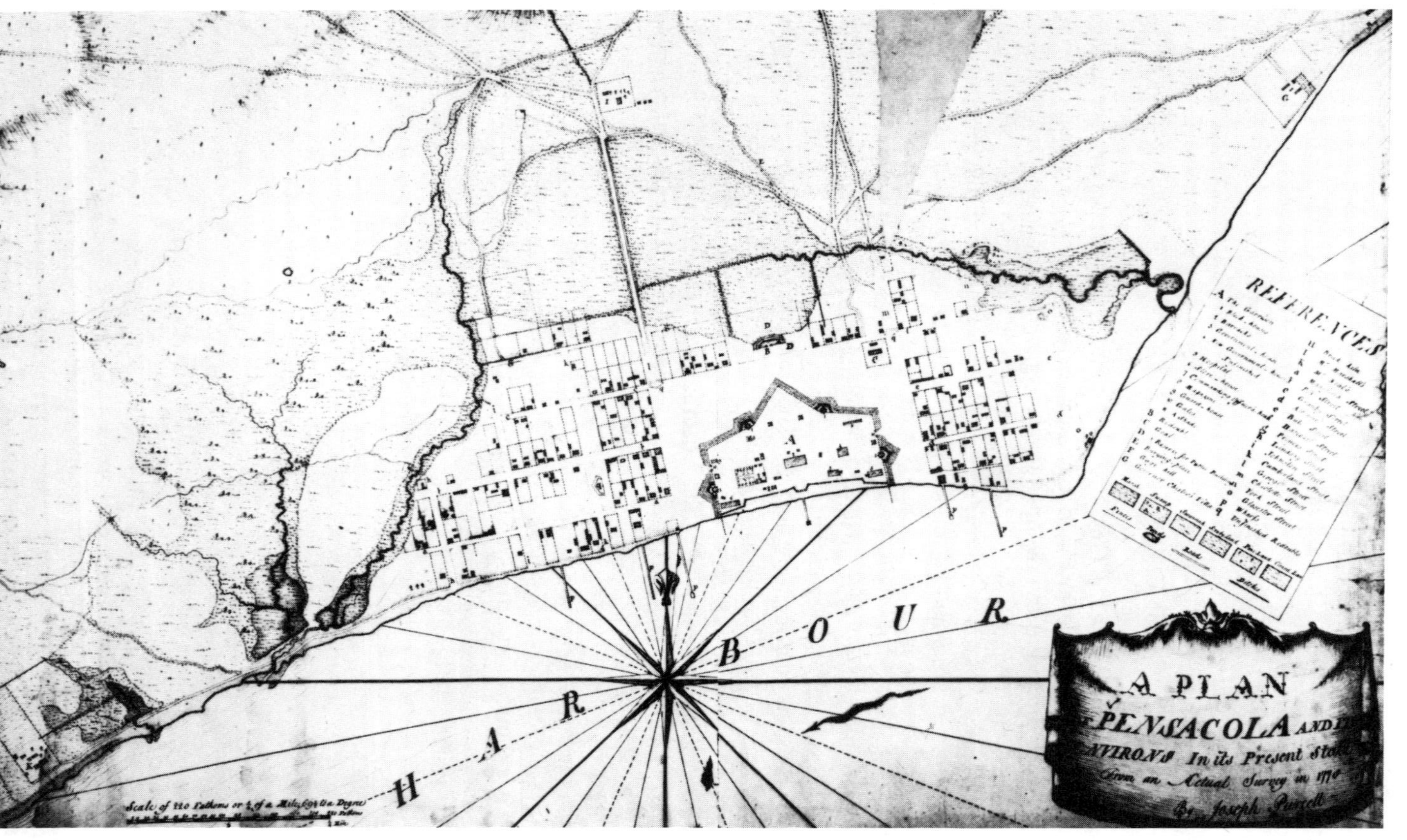

British fortifications at Pensacola in 1780 appear on map by Joseph Purcell: Fort George and the Prince of Wales and Queen's Redoubt located on Gage Hill overlooking the town (top) and the Fort at Pensacola on the bayfront (bottom). Map/Pensacola Historical Society Collections.

British Forts

Name:	Fort at Pensacola
Dates:	1763 — Old Fort San Miguel taken over from Spain. 1781 — Fort of Pensacola returned to Spain.
Location:	Pensacola, between Plaza Ferdinand and Seville Square.
Built By:	Great Britain.
Designed By:	Elias Durnford, Thomas Hutchins, General Frederick Haldimand, and General John Campbell all oversaw construction and renovations of the fort.
Description:	1780 version was five-sided stockade, 1000 by 750 feet, with four two-story blockhouses.
Materials Used:	Logs and sand. Some bricks for buildings within the stockade.
Armament:	Varied from time to time. 1780, most of guns removed to Fort George.
Garrison:	Varied from time to time. Never large.
Present Status:	Ceded to Spain in 1781 intact, as Pensacola had been declared an "open city." A few minor remains have been found. Nothing above ground now.

Name: Fort George

Dates: 1779-1781. Small gun emplacements there earlier.

Location: On Gage Hill, near today's Lee Square, at Palafox and La Rua streets. 1000 yards north of old town.

Built By: Great Britain.

Designed By: Built under the direction of General John Campbell.

Description: Square, eighty yards to a side; demi-bastions at each corner; surrounded by ditch; outer attached hornwork extended southward for 600 yards; casemates in ramparts also served as quarters.

Materials Used: Logs, sand, a few bricks.

Armament: Designed for twenty embrasured guns on parapet.

Garrison: At time of Spanish siege approximately 1100 men in the three forts on Gage Hill.

Present Status: Ceded to Spain, 1781. Renamed Fort San Miguel. Allowed to deteriorate. Small portion excavated and restored as Fort George Park at Palafox and La Rua Streets 1974-76.

Name: Queen's Redoubt.

Dates: 1779-1781.

Location: 600 yards north of Fort George, near today's Spring and Brainard Streets.

Built By: Great Britain.

Designed By: Built under the direction of General John Campbell.

Description: Parapet with protective ditch. Side toward Fort George stockaded.

Materials Used: Timber, logs, sand, and earth.

Armament: Originally designed for four cannon. Parapets later extended for additional cannon.

Garrison: 1100 men in the three forts on Gage Hill.

Present Status: Surrendered to Spanish in 1781. They renamed it Fort San Bernardo and maintained it until 1821. U.S. allowed it to deteriorate. Nothing remains.

Name:	Prince of Wales Redoubt.
Dates:	1780-1781.
Location:	300 yards north of Fort George, near today's Cervantes and Spring Streets.
Built By:	Great Britain.
Designed By:	Built under the direction of General John Campbell.
Description:	Parapet protected by ditches. Shaped somewhat like a hat. 275 feet at its widest point.
Materials Used:	Timber, logs, sand, and earth.
Armament:	Designed for five cannons. Eventually had eight to ten pieces.
Garrison:	1100 men in the three forts on Gage Hill.
Present Status:	Ceded to Spain in 1781. Renamed Fort Sombrero. Allowed to deteriorate. Nothing remains.

Name:	Red Cliffs. Royal Navy Redoubt.
Dates:	1771-1781.
Location:	Naval Air Station, on the Barrancas, approximately where Fort Barrancas now stands.
Built By:	Great Britain.
Designed By:	Site selected by General Frederick Haldimand and Engineer Elias Durnford. They probably provided the plans. General John Campbell directed the repairs in 1780-81. Named it "Royal Navy Redoubt" at that time.
Description:	Upper and lower batteries arranged in shallow v-formation. Had powder magazine and block houses.
Materials Used:	Logs, timber, sand.
Armament:	Haldimand requested eight 24-pounders and sixteen 8-pounders, plus some mortars. Unknown how many were eventually placed there.
Garrison:	Fifty Waldeckers in 1781, plus some reinforcements from the Navy. 140 men at surrender — before then only small garrisons.
Present Status:	Little damaged in siege of Pensacola in 1781. Ceded to Spain. Renamed Fort San Carlos de Barrancas. Nothing remains.

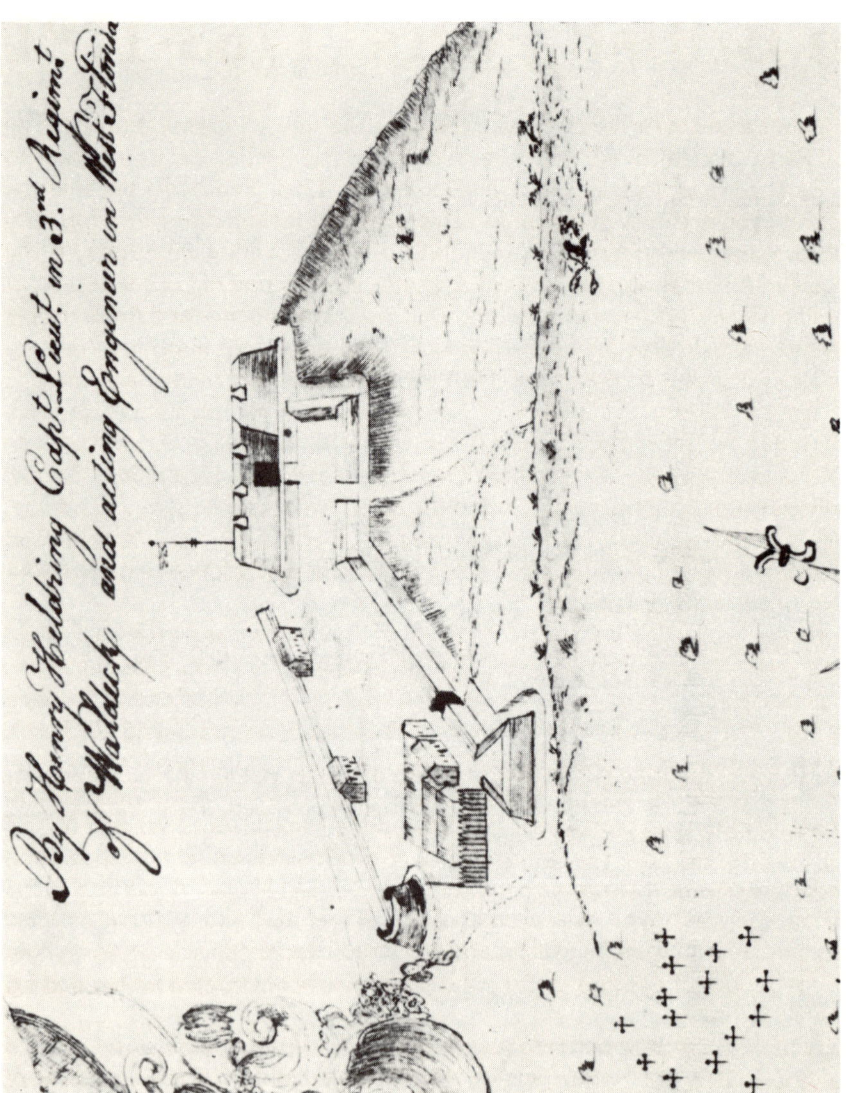

Sketch of British Fort George on Gage Hill in 1780, by Henry Heldring, captain-lieutenant of the 3rd Regiment of Waldeck and acting engineer of British West Florida. Photo courtesy National Archives and Records Service, Record Group 77, Civil Works Map File.

The British Forts, 1763-1781

Once again Pensacola's history was written at the treaty tables in Europe. The Treaty of Paris, signed in 1763, transferred ownership of Florida from Spain to England. By the Royal Proclamation of October 7, 1763, Pensacola became the capital of the Province of West Florida. This province included territory formerly belonging to Spanish Florida and to French Louisiana, covering what today is the southern half of Alabama and Mississippi, the southeastern part of Louisiana (east of the Mississippi River), and northwest Florida to the Chattahoochee and Apalachicola Rivers on the east. Protection of such a large area presented enormous military problems which the British could not solve because of lack of money and men.

As the British military occupation of Pensacola began in the summer of 1763, almost the entire Spanish population of the town left for Havana or Vera Cruz. The post at Pensacola was surrendered by Governor Parrilla to Lieutenant Colonel Augustin Prevost and the third battalion of the Royal American Regiment. This fort, the Spanish San Miguel, had not been well maintained, and the British were shocked by its dilapidation. The palisades were rotting, and the barracks were mere barks huts without fireplaces or windows.[42]

The British promptly embarked on a program to build a town and a fort that would be in keeping with the major colonial province they hoped to develop. Elias Durnford, British engineer and surveyor, laid out a new town plat, which located many of today's streets in the area adjoining present-day Seville Square and Ferdinand VII Plaza, reserving the central section for military use.[43] The military commander, Brigadier Frederick Haldimand, did not arrive in Pensacola until 1767. On his arrival, he found that, in spite of elaborate plans, little had been done to refurbish Fort San Miguel which the British called The Fort at Pensacola.[44] Haldimand lost no time in starting the construction of a new stockade on the site of Fort San Miguel. According to the plan drawing, the new "fort" measured about 1400 feet east and west and 850 feet back from the bay front. Under Haldimand's vigorous leadership, the decaying huts and buildings housing the troops were replaced with well-constructed timber and log structures.[45]

Although their immediate concern was to rebuild and strengthen the defenses of the town, the British did decide in time to erect a small fort at the entrance of Pensacola Bay. Since there was no immediate threat of an attack from the sea, it was not until 1770 or 1771 that Haldimand gave much attention to the defenses of the bay. He and Lieutenant Governor Elias Durnford selected sites for batteries at the western tip of Santa Rosa Island and at the Red Cliffs, as the British termed the Barrancas, on the mainland. Stanley Faye locates this British stockade as "crowning the crest nearly three hundred yards east of the mound that the Spaniards had chosen as a cemetery."*[46] This is approximately where Fort Barrancas now stands. Haldimand included in his defense plans the stationing of two warships at the entrance to the bay; and Governor Chester agreed to send troops from Pensacola to garrison the fort.[47]

In March of 1771, Mr. Flowers, an engineer, reported to the Governor that work on four batteries at Red Cliffs was progressing. A plan of the fortifications, dated March 1771, showed the proposed layout. The defenses consisted of an upper and a lower battery placed in a shallow v-formation. There was a powder magazine and block houses, the latter of which also served to house the troops.[48] The buildings were of wood, and the fascines of the defenses were based on loose, sandy soil. Such construction was not satisfactory because of the time it took to build the fascines, and because such fortifications lasted only a short time without constant repair. All guns that could be spared from the Fort at Pensacola were mounted, but General Haldimand also applied to General Gage, the military commander of the Atlantic and Gulf colonies, for larger caliber cannon.

Mr. Flowers also reported that work had begun on batteries at Tartar Point (on the mainland east of the Red Cliffs) and on Santa Rosa Island. These were to have a powder magazine, a blockhouse in the rear, as well as the mounted guns. An additional blockhouse was to quarter the troops stationed there.

Just how closely these fortifications matched the plan is not known. Haldimand did ask for eight 24-pounders, sixteen 18-pounders, and some large mortars. Records show that troops were stationed there (Red Cliffs) as early as 1771. In 1776 the Council at Pensacola requested the commanding officer to bring the troops from Red Cliffs, Tartar Point, and Santa Rosa Island to Pensacola. A small contingent must have remained at the Red Cliffs, for in March 1777, thirty-one troops were reported there.[49] A report also stated that the batteries were in such poor condition "that it is supposed they would have fallen down with the firing of a few guns."[50]

General Haldimand had left in 1773, and General John Campbell was ordered to take command of the military in British West Florida in 1778.[51] He remained in that position until the surrender to the Spanish in 1781. When he arrived in Pensacola he found the fortifications in very poor repair. The defenses which the British had built earlier had been severely damaged or destroyed by a hurricane in October, 1778.[52] The Spanish by this time were aiding the American colonies in their rebellion against England, and the British in West Florida realized that a confrontation with the Spanish was unavoidable and that Pensacola, as the capital, would certainly be involved. General Campbell immediately began to make plans to strengthen the defenses of Pensacola.[53]

His first concern was the town of Pensacola. The Fort at Pensacola, last renovated by Thomas Hutchins in 1775,[54] now became a large, five-sided stockade of cypress stakes, about ten feet high and with the peak pointing to the north. It extended over 1000 feet along the shoreline and approximately 750 feet inland. Four two-story blockhouses of pine planks were built into the stockade, and it was given additional protection by two advanced redoubts. One redoubt of sand and logs was located north of the stockade on Tarragona Street between Romana and Intendencia Streets. It measured approximately 150 by seventy-five feet, and was protected by a wet ditch. Here cannon were mounted, but it is probable they were later moved into the

Fort George defenses when the Spanish approached.

Another sand and log redoubt was located nearer the bayshore and east of Floridablanca Street.[55] These fortifications would give good protection from an attack on land by troops or Indians armed only with muskets, but would offer little sustained resistance to assault by cannon. The stockade fort had another serious weakness. Just 1200 yards north of the town the ground rose rapidly to about sixty feet above the flood plain. Any hostile force that succeeded in placing cannon and mortars on this nearby height, called Gage Hill, could speedily reduce the fort and town to ruins.[56] When General Campbell arrived in Pensacola there was a small blockhouse, surrounded by a circular double stockade, on Gage Hill. It was decided to build the major defensive works for the town on this height, and work began in 1779 and continued until after the Spanish attack in 1781.[57]

As finally completed on Gage Hill, Fort George, named for the British King,[58] was a square about eighty yards on a side. It was an earth and timber rampart with a demi-bastion at each corner, all surrounded by a dry ditch five to eight yards wide. It had two palisades, one in the ditch and the other beyond the ditch. It was approximately 1000 yards from the town, near present-day Lee Square.

The interior of this fort was a square parade, about twenty-five yards to a side, with doorways opening into rooms built into the rampart. These rooms provided storage and shelter for ammunition and supplies and quarters for the troops. The top of the parapet consisted of planked firing platforms with embrasures for twenty guns.

Because of the sandy soil, revetting was required to maintain the slopes of the parapet, ditch and glacis. This was probably of logs and poles, timber and planking, and perhaps some brick.

An outer attached earthwork (hornwork) extended down the slope of Gage Hill toward the southwest for a distance of about 600 feet. It consisted of two timber and earth ramparts which were separated by about forty yards where they joined the parapet of the main fort, and they widened so that they were about eighty yards apart at the outer enclosed end. This hornwork enclosed three additional gun batteries. Powder magazines, store houses and barracks. It is believed this was constructed to protect the fresh water supply, and it may have provided space in which to hold livestock for food.[59]

While Fort George protected the town, it was vulnerable to attack by guns emplaced on higher ground to the northwest. To forestall such an attack, two redoubts were built, one about 300 yards from Fort George, and a larger redoubt approximately 600 yards from the fort.[60]

The larger work, named the Queen's Redoubt, was built to mount four cannon. It consisted of a parapet six feet high and eighteen feet wide, protected by a ditch twenty-six feet wide and eight feet deep. The front on the Fort George side was stockaded and had a traverse entranceway. This redoubt was further strengthened, after the Spanish had arrived in Pensacola Bay, by adding extended parapets on each side which then curled back to form a crescent redan advanced. Here additional cannon were mounted, making the Queen's Redoubt a formidable obstacle to an attacker approaching from the north.

The smaller redoubt, named the Prince of Wales Redoubt, was designed to mount five cannon, but finally eight or ten pieces were installed. Constructed of timber and earth, as was the Queen's Redoubt, with a parapet protected by a ditch, it measured 275 feet at the widest point. In plan, its shape somewhat resembled a hat which prompted the Spanish to rename it Fort Sombrero in 1783.

During these years, 1779-1781, General Campbell was also concerned about the defenses of Pensacola Bay. He projected a battery on the western end of Santa Rosa Island to complement the repairs he would undertake at the Red Cliffs. Campbell was never able to build a permanent fortification on the island due to the lack of tools, manpower, and guns. Soon after he came to Pensacola, Campbell wrote of his plans to repair the blockhouses and to build magazines, kitchens, and a stockade at the Red Cliffs.[61] Harassed as he was by the lack of skilled workmen and sufficient material, it was not until a year later, in October, 1780, that the general reported that construction at the Red Cliffs had begun.[62] He built a fort of fascines and sand, and he faced it toward Tartar Point intending the fort to prevent enemy occupation of the point only. Later he decided it would be wise to protect the Gulf side also, and he placed a strong battery of five 32-pounders facing in that direction. These 32-pounders were moved from Fort George to the Red Cliffs to complement the six smaller cannon there.[63] This fortification was smaller than the earlier Spanish fort of San Carlos de Austria, but it stood within a ditch and appeared sturdy enough to deter the Spaniards from attacking it once they had reached the mainland.[64] General Campbell named the fort the Royal Navy Redoubt because seamen had done much of the construction, and the navy would garrison and defend the fort in an emergency.[65] The regular garrison consisted of fifty Waldeck soldiers under the command of Major Friedrich Pentzell.[66]

The story of these sailors turned soldiers is one of cooperation and bravery. It had always been the practice of the British to keep several ships in the harbor to defend the entrance to Pensacola Bay. In 1780, General Campbell, recognizing the urgency to strengthen the Pensacola fortifications before the impending Spanish invasion, and finding himself hard pressed for laborers, called upon the crews of these ships for help. The log of HMS *Mentor*, kept by its commander Robert Deans, supplies details of their cooperation. The *Mentor* arrived in Pensacola May 14, 1780, and, within a few days, working parties had been sent to Santa Rosa Island to help construct a battery at its western end. Later parties were sent to the Red Cliffs. At first, some of the sailors, unaccustomed to the extreme heat and the tedium of routine but hard, labor, became unruly; and Commander Deans had to resort to the lash to keep discipline. However, by the time of the Spanish invasion it was reported that the navy contingents were serving well and "cheerfully" under the army commanders.

Since none of the British ships were large enough to challenge the Spanish fleet, their crews were assigned to the land fortifications on Gage Hill and to the Royal Navy Redoubt at the Barrancas. Men from both the *Mentor* and the *Port Navy* served at the Queen's Redoubt; others from the *Port Royal* manned the Prince of Wales Redoubt; while still others from the *Mentor* were at Fort George and the Royal Navy Redoubt. In the explosion at the Queen's Redoubt in May, 1781, seventeen men from the *Mentor* were killed.[67]

The Waldeck regiment had come to Pensacola in early 1780 as part of the reinforcements sent to General Campbell. These German troops were professional soldiers from the Principality of Waldeck, and in coming to Pensacola they were stationed farther south in the American colonies than any of the other German mercenaries. They were not always pleased with the type of soldiering they were called upon to perform. Soon after their arrival they were put to work repairing the defenses on Gage Hill. They found the weather so hot they were forced to work either early in the morning or late at night. They resented the Indians who frequented Fort George, but who did no work, while the English and German soldiers labored at the new defenses being built there. This hornwork was called Fort Waldeck in honor of the Germans. In November, 1780, a group of fifty Waldeck, under Major Pentzell, was sent to the Royal Navy Redoubt where they were still serving when Galvez sailed into Pensacola Bay.[68]

These, then, were the forts and the troops with which the British hoped to repel the Spanish invasion: The Fort at Pensacola, a mediocre stockade in the town proper; the Gage Hill forts, Fort George with its hornwork, the Queen's Redoubt, and the Prince of Wales Redoubt; the Royal Navy Redoubt at the Barrancas; and a battery at Tartar Point. Because of the lack of material and men, General Campbell had abandoned the battery at Point Siguenza on the western end of Santa Rosa Island.[69] These fortifications were manned by approximately 1500 soldiers —[70] regulars, colonial troops, the Waldeckers, friendly Indians, some blacks, and the crews from the British ships.[71]

It was on Santa Rosa Island that the Spanish established their first camp in March of 1781. A few days later, Bernardo de Galvez, the Spanish commander, led his fleet past the guns of the Royal Navy Redoubt. The batteries of the Royal Navy Redoubt fired numerous salvos, but they did little damage to the Spanish fleet as it entered Pensacola Bay. Galvez did not attempt to reduce the Redoubt. He felt that it would be a difficult task to assault it from the land side, and in order to save time and men, he bypassed the fortification and moved inland from Bayou Chico to establish his camp where he could attack Fort George and its redoubts.*[72]

This task was made somwhat easier by the defection of one or two men from the British camp. They revealed the plans of the forts on Gage Hill to General Galvez, and he was able to tailor his attack to take advantage of this information.[73] The smaller British force fought well against the Spanish army, but a direct hit on the magazine at the Queen's Redoubt sealed their fate. The ensuing explosion killed nearly a hundred of the defenders and virtually destroyed the redoubt, making the defense of Fort George impossible. On May 9, 1781, the British forces surrendered to General Galvez. On May 11, a detachment of Spanish soldiers was sent to the Royal Navy Redoubt to take possession of it. The garrison, at that time, numbered 139 men and officers.[74] The battery at Tartar Point had been burned by the British earlier when the Spanish made their landing on the mainland. The Fort at Pensacola remained as it was, for the commanding generals had agreed the town of Pensacola would not be attacked.[75] Its garrison and most of its armament had been taken to Fort George when it was decided to make Gage Hill the chief point of defense.[76]

According to the surrender terms the British soldiers were transported to other American colonies where the British were still in control.[77] A few months later Cornwallis surrendered at Yorktown, and the American colonies gained their independence. Florida, however, because it was once more Spanish territory, had to wait four more decades to become a part of the United States.

* See map for Spanish fortification during the Siege of Pensacola.

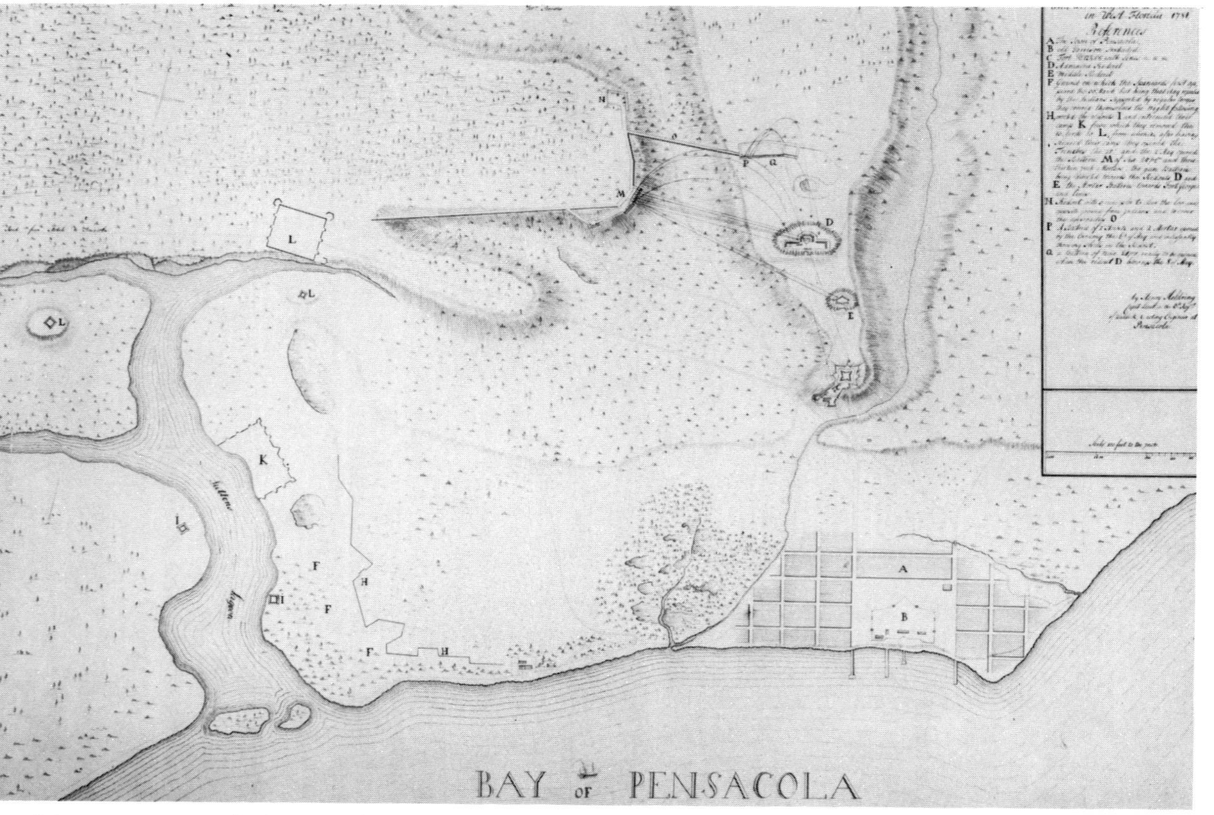

Spanish encampments during 1781 Siege of Pensacola. Sutton's Lagoon (Bayou Chico) is in center and Fort George and the redoubts on Gage Hill are on the right. Field Marshal Bernardo de Galvez's troops landed at the mouth of Sutton's Lagoon and moved inland to his final encampment at Galvez Spring, where the Spanish constructed batteries and trenches for the final assault on the Queen's Redoubt and surrender of the British at Fort George. Photo courtesy William L. Clements Library, University of Michigan.

Later Spanish Forts

Name: San Carlos de Barrancas (former Royal Navy Redoubt)

Dates: 1781, fort ceded to Spain by Great Britain.
1821, fort ceded to United States by Spain.
Remains razed for new Fort Barrancas, 1838.

Location: Naval Air Station where Fort Barrancas now stands. There have been three distinct forts called San Carlos de Barrancas: (1) the renamed British Royal Navy Redoubt; (2) 1797-98 fort, built on the site of old British fort; and (3) 1817 fort, located about 100 yards east of old fort. All overlooked Pensacola Bay.

Built By: Spain.

Designed By: 1798 fort designed by Francisco P. Gelabert.
1817 fort built under the direction of Jose Masot.

Description: 1798: five fronts with one bastion. Sea front paralleled Battery San Antonio. Had palisade and ditch except for side facing the channel.
1817: Small stockade. Walls filled with sand. No bastion or ditch.

Materials Used: Logs, timber, sand.

Armament: 1798: twenty-three cannon on terreplein, 4-, 6-, and 9-pounders.
1817: Ten cannon, 4- to 12-pounders.

Garrison: 1798 — Built for 150 men.
1817. Normally a few troops. At time of surrender to Jackson in 1818, approximately 175 men.

Present Status: Turned over by Spain to United States in 1821. U. S. did little to maintain it. In 1838-1840 razed what little was left to build Fort Barrancas.

Name:	Battery San Antonio (Water Battery)
Dates:	1797 - present
Location:	Naval Air Station, below present Fort Barrancas and facing Pensacola Bay.
Built By:	Spain. Repaired, modernized by United States in 1840s. Restored 1980.
Designed By:	Francisco P. Gelabert.
Description:	Semi-circular works with terreplein and counter-scarp. Three rooms or bombproofs in rear wall (gorge).
Materials Used:	Earth, brick, and stucco.
Armament:	Originally planned for seven guns. Modified and enlarged by United States in 1840s.
Garrison:	Two of the three bombproof rooms were originally built for troop quarters.
Present Status:	Restored by National Park Service, 1978-1980. Administered by Gulf Islands National Seashore. Open to public. Guided tours.

Aerial view of the restored Spanish Water Battery San Antonio (front) and the American-built Fort Barrancas early in the 1980s. The forts were restored by the National Park Service as part of Gulf Islands National Seashore. The water battery San Antonio is sometimes called "Fort San Carlos." Both forts are in the general area of the earlier Fort San Carlos de Barrancas. Photo courtesy of Gulf Islands National Seashore.

The Later Spanish Forts, 1781-1821

The Spaniards, after their victory over the British in 1781, found themselves in possession of a number of forts which, in spite of the recent hostilities, were superior to the ones they had relinquished to the British in 1763. They began their occupation by renaming the forts. Fort George became Fort San Miguel, and Gage Hill, Mount San Miguel. The Prince of Wales Redoubt was named Fort Sombrero because the Spanish thought its shape resembled a hat. This installation was not maintained, and it soon became a minor feature of the terrain. The Queen's Redoubt was repaired and renamed Fort San Bernardo in honor of General Bernardo de Galvez.[78] Out at the Barrancas, the Royal Navy Redoubt became Fort San Carlos de Barrancas "because it was built during the reign of Carlos II."[79] The temporary Spanish trenches, redoubts, and batteries succumbed quickly to the forces of nature. The site of Galvez's major encampment at Galvez Spring on Bayou Chico stood empty. Within the town itself, the stockade of the Fort at Pensacola was indifferently maintained. Gradually, gateways and wagon ports were opened in the palisade to facilitate movement within the town.

Spain's European wars had so depleted her financial resources and her military power that she could spare little of either for Pensacola. In 1786, Governor-General Esteban Miro of Louisiana, who had jurisdiction over West Florida, proposed to station a battalion of infantry at Pensacola, but he found that "no uniforms were available for the members of the Third Battalion, and as an emergency measure the King authorized them to wear captured British 'red coats.' By 1788, however, the battalion had received a shipment of uniforms from Spain."[80]

There was, however, no shortage of plans for the rehabilitation of the forts. Soon after the Spanish returned to Pensacola, two engineers, Gilberto Guillemard and Joaquin de Peramas, presented schemes of defense. Guillemard, who had come with Galvez, drew up elaborate plans for all the forts. Peramas, on the other hand, wanted to concentrate on the town forts. Another plan, favored by the government in New Orleans, recommended abandoning those in town in favor of building forts at the entrance to the bay.[81] With so much disagreement within the administration, little was actually accomplished during the first years of the Spanish occupation.

By 1793 some decision had to be made. Spain was again at war with her European neighbors, and she felt that her colony on the Gulf of Mexico was vulnerable. Adding to the colony's uneasy position was the constant threat of raids by unfriendly Indians stirred up by the restless American frontiersmen looking for new land. The new proposal relied heavily on the earlier survey made by Spanish naval officers soon after

Galvez's victory. These officers had analyzed the failure of the British Royal Navy Redoubt to prevent the entry of the Spanish fleet into the bay, and they had concluded that the redoubt had been placed too high on the bluffs for accurate shelling and too far from the channel to protect it effectively.[82] The 1793 plan for the defense of Pensacola Bay incorporated three projects — a battery at Point Siguenza on the western tip of Santa Rosa Island, a water-level battery at the mainland Barrancas, and a fort above this battery to protect it from a land attack. Of these three projects, only one, the battery at Point Siguenza, was completed.

In 1797 the governing council in New Orleans decided to implement the other portions of the 1793 plan. Don Vicente Folch, the governor at Pensacola, was aware of the vulnerability of the Barrancas to land attack from the rear, and he insisted on a proviso that another fortification be constructed later behind San Carlos de Barrancas for its protection.

Work began on the water-level battery which had been named Battery San Antonio in 1793.[83] Of masonry construction, it was planned as a seven-gun medialuna with a counterscarp. There were three rooms or bombproofs to the rear. One of these was used as a magazine, the other two as storage areas and shelter for the garrison.[84] The structure was stuccoed and embellished with ornamental architectural detailing.[85] In time, it was connected to the upper fortification by a passageway. When San Antonio was built the harbor was much closer to the counterscarp than it is today.[86] The battery was probably designed by Francisco P. Gelabert, who drew a plan for it and also one for Fort San Carlos de Barrancas in 1796. The present form of the battery conforms to this plan.[87]

By 1798 Battery San Antonio had been virtually completed, and work was progressing on the renovation of San Carlos de Barrancas. To protect the water-level battery, Folch chose the site of the old and decaying San Carlos de Barrancas.[88] Unfortunately, the perennial lack of money prevented him from making an entirely new and larger fort. Using Gelabert's sketch of 1796, Edwin C. Bearss describes the fortification: "In laying out this work the Spanish engineer has utilized the parapets and most of the British fort...The fort had five fronts and one bastion. The sea front paralleled the Battery San Antonio gorge [the rear wall] and the bastion faced inland...The superior slope of the parapet of the fronts facing Cemetery Hill to the west and northwest were embrasured. A flight of steps leading down the Barrancas provided communication between San Carlos and San Antonio." A ditch and palisade surrounded the fort except for the side facing the channel. Within the fort on the parade were a subterranean magazine, a guardhouse, and a platform mounting two mortars. The terreplein carried twenty-three cannons, 4-, 6-, and 9-pounders.[89] The fort could accommodate 150 soldiers.[90]

This defense was still flawed. Although the water-level battery, with its counterpart at Point Siguenza and its protection provided for by Fort San Carlos de Barrancas above it, corrected the errors in the British plan, San Carlos itself remained vulnerable to attack from the still higher ground to its rear, for the hornworks and redoubt which Folch thought necessary were never built.[91]

In the first decades of the nineteenth century the size of the Spanish colony on the Gulf of Mexico was drastically reduced. Spain ceded Louisiana to France, who in turn sold the territory to the United States in 1803. All that remained of Spain's great holdings were the provinces of East and West Florida, and Pensacola served as the capital of the latter. The Florida provinces shared a common border with the United States and conflicts soon developed. The Spanish territory became a haven for runaway slaves and a sanctuary and base of operations for Indian raids on Georgian settlements. For much of this period Don Vincente Folch was the governor and commandant (1796-1811). Fortunately, he was clever enough to prevent any serious outbreak of hostilities.

Not all of Folch's problems were at the diplomatic level. He had to concern himself with the day-to-day operations of his colony, worrying about hospital care for his people and wondering why petty crimes had increased at Fort San Carlos de Barrancas. There he uncovered a bootlegging operation conducted by three soldiers. They were selling **aguardiente** (a crude type of rum which was very popular with the troops) to their comrades. He concluded it was the actions of the drunken soldiers which were responsible for the increasing number of fires and robberies. He warned these "entrepreneurs" several times, but no results. Finally Folch ordered that the huts belonging to the soldiers selling the alcohol be torn down, but being a practical man, he had the rum consigned to the post storehouse.[92]

Fighting was common at the garrison, and several soldiers were tried for wounding each other. When sentenced they were confined in jail at the Battery San Antonio, for the casemates of the battery served as a state prison during this time.[93] It seemed a hopeless task to change the opinion of Colonel John Pope, a visitor to Pensacola some years earlier. Pope, commenting on the healthfulness of the city as opposed to the illness so common at the post, reasoned that the soldiers' problems were caused by "inordinate Use of Ardent Spirits and bad Wine, superadded to high seasoned Meats and promiscuous Intercourse with lewd women."[94]

The situation with the United States, already tense, was aggravated by the War of 1812 between the United States and Great Britain. The United States suspected that the Spanish colony was giving aid to the unfriendly Indians. They were certain that the entrance of the British fleet into Pensacola Bay was a hostile act. In August 1814, three British ships under the command of Edward Nicholls sailed into the harbor. 200 troops were landed, and supplies and arms for their Indian allies were unloaded. Nicholls demanded that the Spanish turn over their fortifications to the British and put their troops under his command. Lacking any real strength, the Spanish had to accede to these demands. General Andrew Jackson, who had been authorized by President James Madison to stop Indian raids in the southeast, was in Mobile when he heard of the British occupation. On November 2, he began his march into Florida with 3000 to 4000 soldiers.

The British at that time were installed at Fort San Miguel and Fort San Carlos de Barrancas along with the small Spanish garrisons. They withdrew, however, as Jackson approached Pensacola, for they were reluctant to confront him. When Jackson arrived at Pensacola on November 7, he found only a small Spanish force at San Miguel and in the town of Pensacola. The Spaniards had less than five hundred troops, and these were without discipline or spirit.

The skirmish for the town lasted only a few minutes, but the surrender negotiations were drawn out for so long by the stalling Spanish that all the British troops were able to withdraw to their ships and sail for Fort San Carlos de Barrancas. Jackson could not proceed to the Barrancas until the following day. There he was bitterly disappointed to find that the British had gone. Taking advantage of the surrender delay they had blown up San Carlos de Barrancas, spiked the guns of Battery San Antonio, destroyed the battery at Point Siguenza, and sailed out of the bay.[95] As John Innerarity reported in a letter dated November 10, 1814, "Nothing now remains...but piles of ashes."[96] The statement was an exaggeration written at a time of crisis, but it was true that when the fort was later returned to the Spaniards by the Americans, it was in a wretched condition.

The war ended. The Americans left. But there was another development to add to the problems facing the little community — the threat of raids by privateers. Galveston Bay had become a center of filibusters (privateersmen) preying on the shipping in the Gulf of Mexico. The alarmed population began to prepare a defense for Pensacola. The Spanish commander decided that the town would have to defend itself with its crumbling stockade fort and with gun batteries in the streets. A letter sent from Pensacola at this time (August, 1816), written by John Innerarity to his brother, mentions the construction of three batteries, one at the east end of town, another near Guillemards, and a third to be erected on the heights close to the church. "It is really pleasing," he wrote, "to see the alacrity with which all hands without exception of persons have turned out, working in the water, sand and all kind of labour."[97] The Spanish commander reserved his troops for manning Fort San Carlos de Barrancas and Battery San Antonio.

As a result of the continuing threats from the pirates, a new castillo was constructed at the Barrancas early in 1817. A site was chosen one hundred yards east of the old dilapidated fort and 400 yards east of the cemetery. Stanley Faye describes this new San Carlos de Barrancas as "a work constructed of pine stakes set in parallel lines. Filled with sand the walls formed a thickness of six English feet. No even demi-bastions projected from the stockade. No ditch surrounded this castillo...Ten gun barrels rating from 4- to 12-pounds were mounted within the newer castillo...The fort was so small [that] even in its prime it had offered not enough space for serving more than eight guns at once."[98] This was the fort at Barrancas when Andrew Jackson returned to Florida.

In May 1818, General Jackson and an American army returned to the area. Believing the Spaniards were encouraging the Indians in their attacks on the Americans in Georgia, Jackson took matters into his own hands and marched into Pensacola. His troops occupied the ruined Fort San Miguel. Jose Masot, the Spanish commandant, decided, however, to make his stand at the recently reconstructed Fort San Carlos de Barrancas. He had only twenty-two artillerymen and 153 infantrymen, but he was determined to make some show of resistance. On the twenty-fifth, he aimed the guns of San Carlos de Barrancas and those of Battery San Antonio at the American forces which Jackson had moved to the heights at the Barrancas. After a brief exchange of gunfire Masot surrendered. The Americans established a military government at Pensacola and garrisoned the forts.[99]

Jackson left West Florida shortly after Masot surrendered. Within a few months the United States, deeming it politically wise, returned Pensacola to Spain. However, two interesting reports were made to Jackson by the officers he had left at Pensacola. In August, Captain James Gadsden wrote a general survey of the defenses of

Pensacola. He commented on the good location of San Carlos de Barrancas, its smallness and its need for repairs, and recommended the building of a new work with revetments of masonry to protect the Battery San Antonio. He saw, as had all military men before him, the need of fortifying the western tip of Santa Rosa Island. The Americans left before any of these suggestions could be carried out.[100]

The second document was an inventory of the public buildings in the town of Pensacola. Some of the batteries listed probably were those built at the time of the privateer threat. This inventory names the following defensive works in the town:

On or Around the Public Square:

One brick Guard house.

Four block houses, 31 feet square, two stories high, with brick floors and foundations. One in good order, the rest out of repair.

At the East End of the Town:

One Block house, two stories high, in good order 22 feet square.

One Guard shed of plank, 18 feet long by 12 feet wide.

One four gun Battery of Cypress pickets, filled with sand in bad order, with plank platforms.

At the Head of Palafox Street:

One Block house two stories high, in good order 22 feet square.

At the Foot of Palafox Street:

One Block house, two stories high, in good order, 22 feet [square]

One four gun Battery of Cypress pickets filled with sand in good order, with plank platform.

At the West End of the Town:

One Block house two stories high, in good order, 22 feet square.

One four gun Battery of Cypress pickets filled with sand, in good order, with plank platform.

Five Sentry boxes, and one flag staff.[101]

It had long been evident that Spain could not maintain her colony in Florida, and in 1821 she ceded the territory of Florida to the United States. Andrew Jackson was sent to take over the government from the Spaniards. On July 17, 1821, surrender ceremonies took place in the Plaza at Pensacola, and Jackson received the territory from Colonel Callava. Later in the day Jackson sent four companies of infantry under Major James E. Dinkins to take possession of Fort San Carlos de Barrancas and Battery San Antonio. (There were no usable forts left in town or on Mount San Miguel.)[102] At the Barrancas there was a small parade, the Spanish flag was lowered as the American flag was raised. When both were at half mast, they were saluted by the Spanish, after which the Spanish flag was lowered and the American flag was raised and saluted by the United States troops.[103]

Thus ended a hundred years of Spanish presence in Pensacola Bay. Of all the trenches dug, palisades erected and cannons emplaced there remains today only the Battery San Antonio. It is one of the few examples of early Spanish military architecture still in existence in the United States, and it is the oldest surviving fortification in the Pensacola area.

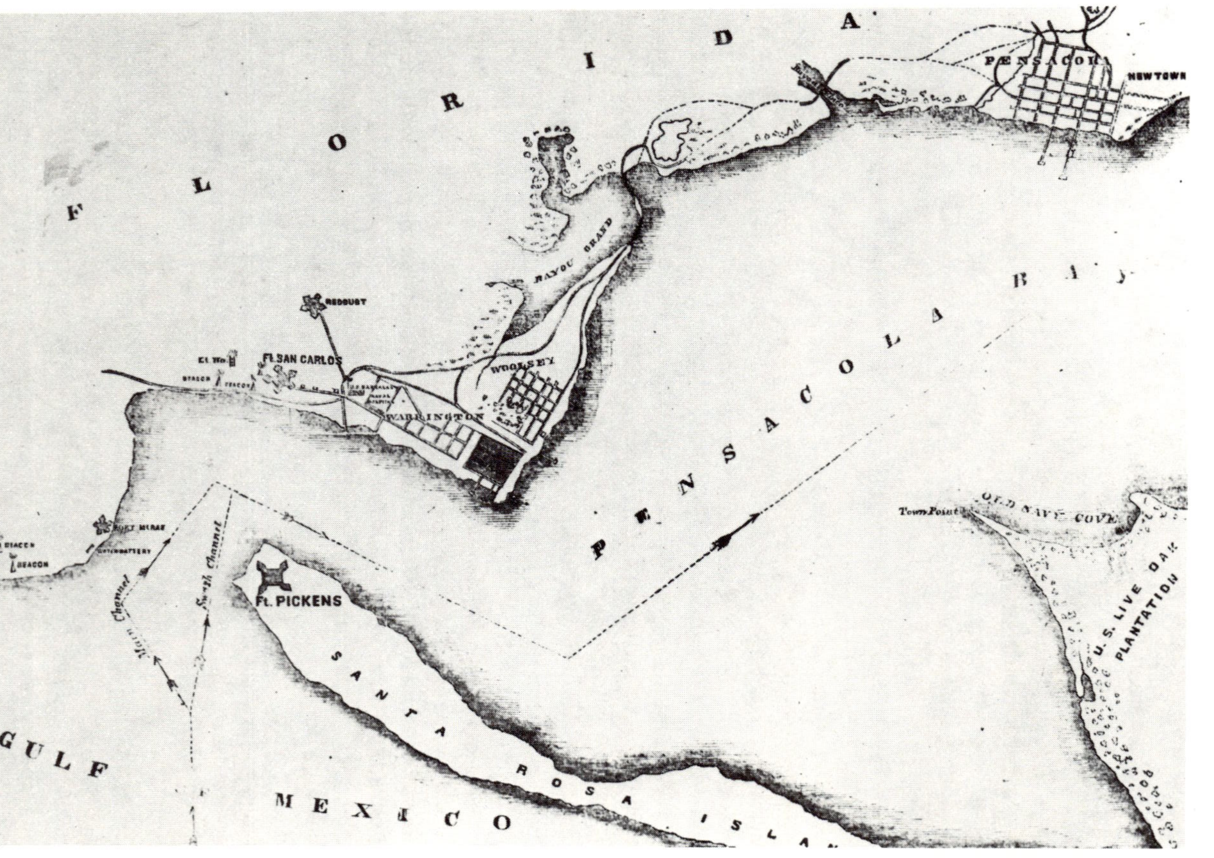

Civil War harbor map from Harper's Weekly, *February 9, 1861, shows military fortifications and the town of Pensacola as Federal troops at Fort Pickens faced Confederate forces occupying mainland forts and the Navy Yard.* Map/Pensacola Historical Society Collections.

American Forts: The Building Years, 1821-1861

When the United States acquired Florida in 1821, the Spanish fortifications at Pensacola were in bad shape. The stockade in the town had fallen into ruins and the gun batteries and blockhouses, the only defensive works still standing, had not been maintained. On Mount San Miguel north of Pensacola, Forts San Miguel and San Bernardo likewise showed the result of long neglect. The siege works and redans constructed by General Galvez in 1781 were completely useless. Forts San Carlos de Barrancas and Battery San Antonio at the Red Cliffs (Barrancas) were in better condition for the Spanish had repaired much of the damage done by the departing British in 1814, but they had not replaced the battery at Point Siguenza on Santa Rosa Island which the British had destroyed. Pensacola and its Bay were without effective defenses with which to oppose a determined aggressor attacking by land or sea.

The American soldiers who came to garrison Pensacola initially occupied the Spanish barracks in the town and at Fort San Carlos de Barrancas. When, in 1822, yellow fever appeared among the civilian population, the troops moved to Galvez Spring, and there began construction of a camp which was named Cantonment Clinch at ceremonies on July 4, 1823.[104]

In 1825, the War Department ordered Colonel Clinch to move all wagons and stores belonging to the Army from the Barrancas to Cantonment Clinch and Fort San Carlos de Barrancas was transferred to the Navy.[105]

The Army did not build any permanent defensive fortifications until the recommendation of the Bernard Board were acted on beginning in the 1830s.[106] The Bernard Board had been established by the United States Government in 1817. As early as 1822, this Board began to prepare plans for the permanent defenses of Pensacola. When, in 1825, Pensacola was selected as the site of the Gulf Coast Navy Yard, this process was given added emphasis.[107]

As finally developed the fixed defenses of Pensacola Bay were to consist of three forts: one on the western tip of Santa Rosa Island, a second on Foster's Bank immediately opposite to the west, and a third on the mainland bluff near the site of the old Spanish San Carlos de Barrancas. This placed it above and behind the Spanish Battery San Antonio which came to be designated as the Water Battery.[108]

The first two forts commanded the water approach to the harbor while the third on the height (Barrancas) protected the Navy Yard on the east and the land approaches from the north and west. As this last fort was exposed to high ground on the north a redoubt was to be built approximately three-quarters of a mile inland as protection against a land attack on either the fort or the Navy Yard. A line of earthworks would extend from this fort to the Redoubt to guard the intervening space.[109]

These structures, which were named respectively Fort Pickens, Fort McRee, Fort Barrancas, and Barrancas Redoubt, were built in that order between 1829 and 1859, largely under the supervision of Captain (later Major) William H. Chase, U. S. Corps of Engineers.[110] Of brick masonry construction, they incorporated the latest principles for fixed defenses and siege warfare as developed in the nations of the Old and New World, whose navies at that time consisted of wooden sailing ships armed with smooth-bore cannon, firing round projectiles at effective ranges of about one mile.

The important construction materials needed, with the exception of sand, seashells and timber, were not obtainable in the Pensacola area. Bricks were initially shipped in from the Mobile brick yards. Captain Chase, knowing that the clay deposits in the Pensacola area were of high quality, urged local businessmen to set up kilns, and after several abortive trials Pensacola firms succeeded in producing bricks with the dimensional control and quality required.[111]

Sandstone, lime (in later years, cement), granite, slate, large iron fittings, sheet lead, bitumen, cordage and leather had to be shipped in. A procurement office in New York was used for items not obtainable on the Gulf Coast and it took months after an order had been placed for supplies to arrive.[112]

Initially, skilled labor was scarce. The manpower used to build the forts was slave labor supplied by contractors who in turn hired them from slaveholders in Pensacola and Mobile.[113]

The first fort completed was Pickens, and although not yet armed, it was garrisoned by an artillery company of thirty-four men in October, 1834. Their stay was brief, for in December the company was moved to Fort Brooke on Tampa Bay. In May, 1835, another artillery company arrived at Fort Pickens, but the outbreak of the second Seminole War caused the War Department to move this company in November, 1835, and Fort Pickens was left in the care of guards hired by the Quartermaster Department.[114]

This was a pattern that was to be repeated at each of the forts right up to the outbreak of the Civil War. The United States did not have enough soldiers to man all of the fortifications being built. Occupancy of the Pensacola forts by garrison troops was intermittent, both before and after the period of the Civil War.[115]

Meanwhile (1834) construction had begun on Fort McRee on Foster's Bank. As was the case with Pickens, it was first necessary to build a wharf at which to receive materials, and to lay a narrow gauge rail line from the wharf to the construction site. Small cars pulled by mules were used to transport the materials. Wooden buildings for quarters, shops, storage and the stables were then constructed and work could proceed on the fort.

Neither Pickens nor McRee received the full complement of guns called for in the original plan immediately upon occupation by troops. The first guns put in place at

Fort Pickens were sixteen 24-pounders mounted in the casements in the Fall of 1835.[116] Arming of the forts proceeded at a slow pace, continuing right up until the outbreak of the Civil War.

Construction of Fort Barrancas began in 1839 and was virtually completed by 1844, while construction of the redoubt got underway in 1845, was interrupted for four years, 1851-54, and finally ended short of completion in 1859.

Maps of Foster's Bank dated 1852 and 1860 show a battery placed just south of McRee, labeled "Advanced Battery" in 1852, and "South Battery" in 1860. One map indicates that this was a brick structure and it is probable that this was a water level battery. Maps of the Civil War period do show a "Water Battery" in the same location.[117]

When these forts were designed the engineers expected that the garrison would be housed within the forts, using the casemates for quarters, kitchens, and storage. There is no record of other quarters being constructed for the garrisons of Forts Picken and McRee.

When the war with Mexico ended in 1848, a battalion of the 4th U. S. Artillery was sent to occupy Forts Pickens and McRee. On their arrival the officers were shocked at the sight of the casemate quarters. The Battalion commander convened a board of his company commanders "to examine and report upon the state and condition of Forts Pickens and McRee, with reference to their being occupied by troops." The officers found the works unfit in their present condition for occupation by the troops. They observed that at neither post were there any facilities for the sick, for cooking, washing or for storing supplies. The casemates which were to serve as barracks were occupied by mounted guns. "They possess none of the qualities that are usually supposed to belong to the residence of men in a respectable community..." The Board report stated that Forts Pickens and McRee might be occupied by one company each, "but not with a due regard to their health, discipline, or respectability." The Battalion surgeons agreed with the Board's report and urged that immediate measures be taken toward improvement.

The Battalion commander, Lieutenant Colonel John V. Gardner, was especially irked when he compared the cold, damp casemates in the forts with the quarters enjoyed by the sailors and marines at the nearby Navy Yard, and he complained about it bitterly in a letter: "this difference in facilities provided by the government 'between the two great branches of its martial services, as everywhere seen, and here most painfully felt.' "

The Battalion had arrived in November, 1848. In early 1849, the War Department decided to re-deploy it, and the last companies departed in August leaving the Pensacola forts again under Major Chase and maintained by Ordnance sergeants.[118]

These and other complaints about the troop facilities at the forts resulted in an appropriation for construction of permanent barracks at the Barrancas. By November, 1850, one block had been completed and was ready for occupancy. From that time until early 1861, no troops were regularly garrisoned in the forts. Units assigned to the defense of Pensacola Harbor were quartered at Barrancas Barracks, from where fatigue parties and guard details were sent to look after the police and security of the forts.[119]

None of the forts received the full complement of guns originally planned. As time passed new developments caused the War Department to order heavier guns for seacoast defense.[120] This often required the redesign of gun carriage platforms and foundations which also required structural modifications to the forts. At the onset of the Civil War not one of the forts was completely armed.

As with any structure that man builds which is constantly exposed to the elements, the Pensacola fortifications required continuous maintenance. Even before the fort was completed a part of the wall of Pickens had to be rebuilt. Foundations shifted, walls leaned, the wind and rain washed away the sand parapet platforms; wood, rope and leather rotted, and iron rusted. Water leaked into the casemates and interior chambers. This proved to be a problem that was never completely eliminated. While annual appropriations for maintenance kept the forts structurally solid, none was in "fighting trim" when in January, 1861, they became the objective of the newly emerging Confederate states.

It was in 1829 that the first construction stake was driven into the sands of Santa Rosa Island to mark the location of Fort Pickens. Thirty years were to pass before the work ended. Major William H. Chase had been the Engineer Officer in charge of the construction program for 25 years, having been transferred to Key West in 1854.[121] These years were filled with periods of intense activity alternating with intervals of little progress. The pace of the work was governed largely by appropriations of funds by the Congress, always subject to the varying winds of domestic politics and international relations.

As funds ran low the construction force would be reduced or the work stopped entirely until a new appropriation bill was passed. Then workers would be recalled, materials ordered, and activity resumed, subject always to the vagaries of the weather and the ever-present threat of yellow fever. It is not surprising that so many years would pass before the program was completed.

Designed by the Corps of Engineers, these forts exhibit a quality of architectural design and simplicity that states their purpose unequivocally. Remarkably free of any kind of non-essential ornamentation, they were and still are models of the ethic of the American frontier where function is more important than form. As engineering works, the forts were well built with careful attention to the details. Furthermore, it does not appear that the funds appropriated were squandered and no hint of scandal has come to light. While Major Chase did sometimes anticipate the passage of an appropriations bill by the Congress, it would appear that the work accomplished under his direction, and under the officers who succeeded him, was carefully done with a degree of skill and care that is to their credit.

Although the forts were not subjected to the ultimate test, an attack by an invading army and navy, they did accomplish the purpose for which they were built; i.e., as passive defenses of an important Gulf Coast harbor. In addition, the construction program contributed materially to the economy of Pensacola for more than a generation. The **Pensacola Gazette** in March 29, 1845, published this list of the cost of the Pensacola forts:

Fort Pickens	$740,000
Fort McRee	335,000
Fort Barrancas	334,000
Advanced Redoubt	150,000

However, 1860 brought a set of circumstances not foreseen by the planners of the defense of Pensacola Bay. For eighty-five years the United States had located its coastal defenses so as to oppose aggressors coming from over the seas, but now domestic events were moving toward a climactic act that would divide the country and have American armies attacking the Pensacola forts from the homeland.

Major William H. Chase, U.S. Army engineer who supervised the building of Pensacola's American fortifications. Photo courtesy Special Collections, John C. Pace Library, University of West Florida.

Lieutenant Adam J. Slemmer, First U.S. Artillery, evacuated Federal troops from Fort Barrancas and commanded Fort Pickens while awaiting Union reinforcements. Harper's Weekly, February 23, 1861/Pensacola Historical Society Collections.

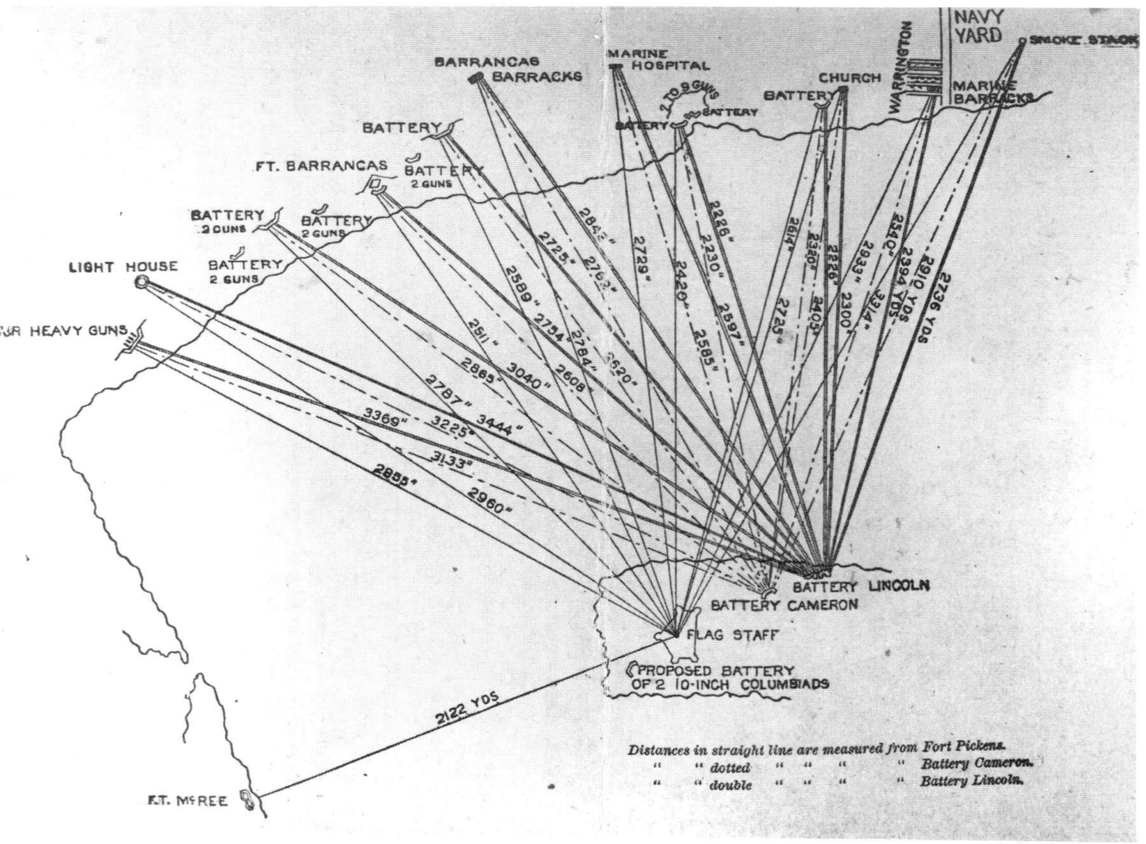

Union and Confederate batteries and firing distances across Pensacola Bay, probably November, 1861. All distances are shown in yards. Map courtesy Gulf Islands National Seashore.

American Forts: The Fighting Years, 1861-1865

The election of the Republican candidate as President in November, 1860, demonstrated clearly the division in the country as Mr. Lincoln did not receive a single electoral vote from a Southern state. South Carolina voted to secede from the Union in December, 1860, and all indications were that Florida, Alabama and the other Southern states would follow the same course. Officers and soldiers manning the military installations in the South found themselves caught up in the rush of events destined to involve them no matter where their symphathies lay.

The outgoing Buchanan Administration had done nothing to reinforce the garrison at Pensacola or to ready the forts for defense. The Commanding Officer at Pensacola and his second in command had been permitted to go on leave and the crisis found thirty-one year old First Lieutenant Adam J. Slemmer in command of the one company of Field Artillery then stationed at Pensacola. The portrait of Lieutenant Slemmer shows a studious looking man peering at the camera through steel rimmed spectacles. Indeed he had served for four years as a professor at the Military Academy, but Lieutenant Adam Slemmer proved to be a man of action. Before he had received instructions from Washington he began to take steps to protect the government property from a rumored take-over by the Florida State Militia.

On January 5, 1861, it was learned that Alabama State troops had seized Fort Morgan on Mobile Bay. Slemmer and his second in command, Second Lieutenant Jeremiah H. Gilman, conferred with Commodore James Armstrong, Commandant of the Navy Yard. As neither had received instructions from Washington to guide them, the conference was inconclusive. Nevertheless, Slemmer began to consolidate arms at Fort Barrancas, and on January 8 had moved part of his company from barracks into Fort Barrancas. There gun batteries were put in working order, guard details established and at night the draw-bridge leading into the fort was raised.

About midnight on the eighth a group of men approached the fort and failing to answer when challenged, were fired upon by the guard. The alarm was sounded as the group retreated in the darkness in the direction of Warrington. Slemmer doubled the guard and they waited through the night to see if another attempt would be made to take possession of the fort. These were the first shots fired by the Federals in the Civil War.[122]

On the ninth, the Washington mail brought instructions to take all possible measures to protect the forts from seizure and to consult with the commander of the

Navy Yard. When they met again Armstrong had also received instructions from Washington. The two Army men insisted that, with the limited means at their disposal, only one of the forts could be held and Fort Pickens was chosen. Armstrong then agreed to make two ships available to move the men and material to the island fort. The two ships were the armed steamer, *Wyandotte*, commanded by Lieutenant Otway H. Berryman and the storeship, *Supply*, commanded by Lieutenant Commander Henry Walke.

On January 9, a part of Slemmer's command boarded the *Supply* and was ferried to Fort Pickens where the artilleries began to mount the guns and make necessary preparations for defense. There was plenty to be done as the fort had not been garrisoned for ten years.

On January 10, all of Slemmer's company and thirty-one seamen from the Navy Yard were ferried to Santa Rosa Island with most of the powder and all of the fixed ammunition and other supplies taken from Forts McRee and Barrancas. The guns bearing on the channel were spiked by the departing Federals.

The force left to hold the Navy Yard numbered thirty-eight marines and thirty sailors. With the evacuation of the mainland forts it could not be defended. On January 12, Florida militia under Colonel Tennant Lomax, variously estimated at from 300 to 800 men, moved into the vicinity and demanded the surrender of the yard. Faced with such odds Commodore Armstrong surrendered the yard and the United States flag was hauled down and the flag of Florida hoisted in its place. For this action Commodore Armstrong was later courtmartialed.[123]

At this time the only United States vessels in the harbor were *Wyandotte* and *Supply* which were commanded by men loyal to the Union. The *Wyandotte* took *Supply* in tow and moved out of the Bay and so they were retained by the Federal forces.

In the afternoon of January 12, three officers of the militia, accompanied by an employee from the Navy Yard who was acquainted with Lieutenants Slemmer and Gilman, went to the island and walked to the fort, demanding admittance. The guard sent for Slemmer and when the visitors stated they had been sent by the governors of Florida and Alabama to demand a peaceable surrender of the fort, Slemmer refused. The visitors departed and that night a strong guard was mounted, but there was no attack on the fort.

Slemmer continued to drive his men to improve the defenses of the fort. It was an overwhelming task for the fort had been so long inactive. Lumber, tools and cordage were in short supply as the hasty departure had not given time to strip the mainland forts of all needed items. Slemmer had the foresight to bring a mule and cart to help with moving the heavy loads, but after a few days the mule waded into the Bay, swam back to the mainland, and deserted the Union cause.

There is little doubt that a determined assault by the South could have overwhelmed the little garrison and taken Fort Pickens. Before the Secessionists could decide on such a course of action, a truce was arranged by Stephen Mallory, then U.S. Senator from Florida (later the Confederate Secretary of the Navy), and President James Buchanan, stipulating that reinforcements would not be landed by the Federals, provided that no attempt was made by the South to capture the fort. This truce held until President Lincoln, after his inauguration, decided to reinforce

Fort Pickens and reinforcements were landed in April.[124]

Both sides strengthened their forces through the summer of 1861. The Confederates, commanded by General Braxton Bragg, ringed the shore from the Navy Yard to the Fort McRee Water Battery with eighteen batteries of guns and mortars. These were in addition to the guns mounted in Forts McRee and Barrancas and the Barrancas Water Battery. Constructed of timber and sand bags all of these batteries were positioned to fire at Fort Pickens.[125]

The Santa Rosa Island troop camps were set up, additional batteries mounted on the shore, and the guns of Fort Pickens repositioned to fire on the mainland installations. The Union commander at this time was Colonel Harvey Brown.

On October 9, 1861, the Confederates made a night landing on Santa Rosa Island with about 1,000 men under command of General Richard H. Anderson. The advancing Confederate troops surprised and overran Camp Brown located east of Fort Pickens, scattering the men of the Sixth New York Volunteers. Reinforcements from the fort stopped the Confederate advance, and the Southerners then retreated to the landing site where they reboarded the boats and returned to the mainland.[126]

The Union response to the Battle of Santa Rosa Island, as the surprise attack was called, was to bombard the Confederate positions on the mainland. Two Federal warships, the *Niagara* and the *Richmond*, participated and were particularly effective against Fort McRee and the Fort McRee Water Battery, both of which were badly damaged.

The first bombardment which took place on November 22 and 23 was followed by another on January 1, 1862. The second bombardment involved only the land batteries of Fort Pickens and the mainland. The towns of Woolsey and Warrington to the north and west of the Navy Yard were burned and the Navy Yard was also damaged. However, the Union forces were not strong enough to mount an assault on the Confederate mainland positions. The New Year found the opposing forces glaring at each other across the blue waters of the bay.[127]

Meanwhile the tide of battle had turned against the Confederates in other theatres of the War and the need for troops forced them to evacuate Pensacola, and on May 10, 1862, the U. S. flag was again raised over the mainland forts.[128]

Pensacola and its military installations were held by the Union for the rest of the war. Fort Pickens continued as the main defense for the harbor entrance and later in the War was also used as a prison and detention area for military and civilian prisoners.

Fort McRee, which had been so badly damaged in the two bombardments, and further damaged by fires set by the evacuating Confederates, was not repaired.

Forts Barrancas and Redoubt were strengthened and manned until the war ended, but neither saw any action of consequence for the rest of the war.

Interior walls of Fort Pickens on Santa Rosa Island, circa 1900. Photo/Pensacola Historical Society Collections.

East side of the old neglected Advanced Redoubt of Barrancas, known locally as "Fort Redoubt." Bliss Quarterly, *1897, featured this photo of the redoubt that was the first Pensacola harbor fortification restored by the National Park Service as part of Gulf Islands National Seashore.* Photo/Pensacola Historical Society Collections.

American Forts: The Years of Change, 1866-1980

After peace came the Army garrisons at Pensacola shrank rapidly as demobilization proceeded. The last garrison soldiers moved from Santa Rosa Island in 1867,[129] and except for periods of training or crisis, the Pensacola forts were virtually neglected. Funds appropriated for maintenance and repairs dwindled and the years that passed saw the structures deteriorating.

Because of the recurring outbreaks of yellow fever in the hot months, the War Department adopted the practice of removing all except caretaker troops from Fort Barrancas during the period from July to November. On occasion the move would be to a temporary camp on Santa Rosa Island or to a location north of Bayou Grande. In other years the troops were sent to permanent Army posts in Alabama or Georgia.[130]

The last decade of the century found the Pensacola forts badly run-down. A report made by the Engineer officer dated July, 1890 stated that, "leakage through the casemate arches and walls — " of Forts Pickens and Barrancas had become so general that it is "useless to expend any further money in attempting to preserve these forts."[131]

For twenty years after the Civil War America neglected its seacoast system. However, in the 1880s a growing awareness among the electorate caused President Grover Cleveland, in 1885, to convene a board headed by the Secretary of War, William C. Endicott, to review the defense situation.[132]

The report of the Endicott Board became the basis for an extensive rebuilding of America's seacoast defense system. The old forts, however, had outlived their time.

Masonry forts had always been vulnerable to siege guns on land which could be directed to fire with sufficient accuracy against a small area of a wall to breach it by repeated battering. On the other hand, smooth-bore naval cannon fired from moving vessels lacked the precision to shatter masonry in this cumulative fashion. The appearance of rifled cannon changed this situation.

The introduction of large numbers of rifled cannon during the Civil War, even the primitive muzzle-loading varieties, soon demonstrated that such guns could accomplish with a relatively few rounds what smooth-bore cannon would achieve only after a sustained bombardment. This and other advances in the equipment for warfare were considered by the Endicott Board with the result that the Pensacola forts became merely an adjunct of the twentieth-century defense system.

In the waning years of the nineteenth century, two 15-inch Rodman guns were mounted just below the Water Battery at Barrancas to be used for training purposes. These guns and those remaining in the forts were hastily activated at the time of the Spanish-American War but that period of urgency was soon over. The year 1900 found three 8-inch Rodman rifles still in place in Fort Barrancas and in condition to be used for training. When the Endicott System batteries on Santa Rosa Island and Foster's Bank were ready, there were used for the training and the old guns peered forlornly across the Bay as they listened to the roar of the younger generation.[133]

In 1901 Congress fixed the organization of the Army at fifteen regiments of cavalry, thirty regiments of infantry, and a Corps of Artillery which was to consist of two branches, Coast Artillery and Field Artillery. The Congress had recognized seacoast artillery as a "distinct branch of service" whose officers and men must be specialists to a greater degree in handling heavy ammunition, fire control, and night-time harbor illumination. The Coast Artillery would be responsible for the care and use of the fixed and movable elements of land and coast fortifications, including the submarine and torpedo defenses.[134]

Fort Barrancas became a Coast Artillery post and the Headquarters for the coastal defenses of Pensacola. As such it became one of the major Coast Artillery training bases in the South. New recruits, the National Guard, the Citizens Military Training Corps, and the Reserve Officers Training Corps all came to the shores of Pensacola Bay to learn to handle the modern weapons installed there.[135] The Post of Barrancas was to continue in this role until deactivated in 1947.

During World War I the pace of training was greatly increased as a number of coast artillery guns were sent to Europe, and Barrancas was to supply some of the guns and the crews.[136]

The years between the two World Wars brought a lull in activity, but even during the depression years the Army's role as instructor for the CMTC and ROTC continued, and Barrancas remained an active post.

When the Civilian Conservation Corps was organized in 1933, Fort Barrancas became headquarters of a district and was responsible for 5,000 men in twenty-two locations in four states.[137]

About this time the Public Works Administration was organized, and new base facilities were constructed at many Army posts including Barrancas. When the Works Progress Administration was set up, one local project was the stabilization and restoration of old Fort Barrancas, the Water Battery and the Advanced Redoubt.[138]

World War II saw the peak of the Army's role in Pensacola. Perfection of long-range bombing, carrier-based air fleets, and the development of rocket missiles rendered fixed coastal defenses obsolete. Fort Barrancas was deactivated in April, 1947, and the physical plant was transferred to the Navy to become a part of the Naval Air Station.[139]

An Act of Congress passed in 1948 transferred the old forts to the Department of Interior, which then turned Pickens over to the Florida Board of Parks and Historic Memorials. The state built a road from Pensacola Beach to the site of the fort and maintained a state park there until 1971. Fort Barrancas, the Water Battery, and the Redoubt continued to waste away as the years of neglect took their toll.[140]

In 1971, an Act of Congress established the Gulf Islands National Seashore as a part of the National Park Service. Under this new ownership a great amount of stabilization and restoration has been completed at all the forts. Today, rehabilitated, they stand as impressive monuments of the military history of Pensacola.[141]

Cantonment Clinch

The site of Cantonment Clinch near Galvez Spring has been the campground for Spanish and American soldiers on several occasions. The Spanish under General Galvez camped at this locale while besieging Fort George in 1781. When General Jackson came to Pensacola to accept the transfer of the Floridas to the United States in 1821, a part of his troops camped here.[142]

Sometime in 1822, the American soldiers that were garrisoned in Pensacola moved to Galvez Spring, which they called Camp Hope (some sources give "Camp New Hope"). Also in 1822, the American soldiers camped in the vicinity of Fort San Carlos de Barrancas, to escape the yellow fever epidemic among the civilians, moved to the vicinity of Camp Hope and set up a temporary camp called Camp Brady. In April, 1823, the two camps were merged and designated Camp Galvez Spring. Subsequently, at ceremonies on July 4, 1823, the camp was named Cantonment Clinch in honor of the troop commander, Colonel Duncan L. Clinch.

There is a brief description of this camp as seen by Karl Bernhard, Duke of Saxe-Weimer-Eisenbach.[143] He came to Pensacola from Mobile in January, 1825, and at the invitation of Colonel Clinch, attended an inspection of the troops and toured the camp. He described it as having a large open area or parade ground with a row of ten long houses that shared a continuous roof on one side and individual houses lining the other side in which the company officers lived. At one end of the parade ground was a two story wooden house for the camp commander, and at the other, a wooden house used as the post hospital. According to Bernhard the complement of the camp at the time of his visit was about twenty soldiers and four officers including Colonel Clinch and the Regimental Surgeon.

In May, 1825, the War Department instructed Colonel Clinch to move all Army personnel and stores from the Barrancas to Cantonment Clinch as Fort San Carlos de Barrancas was to be turned over to the Navy.

One source indicates that the camp was closed about 1829; however, other records indicate that the hospital at the camp was used by the Navy until the hospital building at the Navy Yard was completed.

The site is now largely a Pensacola residential area located between Jackson and "Z" Streets and the northern arm of Bayou Chico.

Fort Pickens

Name: Fort Pickens

Dates: 1829 to present.

Location: Western end of Santa Rosa Island.

Built By: United States Corps of Engineers.

Designed By: Brigadier General Simon Bernhard. Major William H. Chase was the on-site engineer.

Description: Five sided plan with five bastions, of brick masonry construction. Had guns in casemates and barbette. Surrounded by a wide moat, and on the eastern front was protected by a high counter scarp wall. The perimeter of the walls measured 900 yards.

Materials Used: 21,500,000 bricks, earth, granite, slate, wood and metal (iron fittings and lead sheeting), bitumen.

Armament: Designed for 200 cannon (24- and 32-pounders), twenty mortars and twenty-eight carronades. One tier of guns in casemates and one tier in barbette.

Artist's conception of Fort Pickens on Santa Rosa Island from the Gulf side in 1861. Sketch from Frank Leslie's Illustrated Newspaper, *February 9, 1861, shows two tiers of sally ports instead of the actual single tier.* Sketch/Pensacola Historical Society Collections.

Fort Pickens: The Early Years, 1829-1860

When selected in 1829, the site of Fort Pickens was much nearer the channel it was to guard than it is today. Old drawings show that the wall of the fort facing the channel was located about two hundred yards from the water's edge.[144]. In the intervening years the action of wind and waves has combined to cause the island to grow almost three-quarters of a mile to the west, putting the fort a considerable distance from the present channel. Likewise, Foster's Bank on the other side of the channel has been eroded away and the site of Fort McRee is now under water.

Fort Pickens was named for Brigadier General Andrew Pickens of the South Carolina State Troops in the American Revolution.[145] When constructed it was a five-sided figure with two of the sies, which met an an oblique angle, facing the channel. The fort had one tier of casemates and a barbette tier for cannon. A bastion at each of the five corners provided for enfilading fire along the face of the walls from casemated guns.

The level of the parade was seven feet above high tide, placing the terreplein on which the barbette guns were positioned, twenty-eight and one half feet above the high tide marker. The walls of the fort measured approximately forty feet high from the bottom of the moat, and varied in thickness from three to twelve feet. Today the moat has been filled in some five or six feet of its depth, so the walls are not seen to be as high as when constructed.[146]

When completed in 1834, the fort was surrounded by a dry moat from fifty to one hundred feet wide and a glacis which varied in height and extent.

The east front, different in design from the other fronts, was to defend against assaulting troops approaching by land. This wall, which was 231 yards long, was protected by a high glacis extending in a sweeping curve or bonnet around the bastions at either end. This east front wall which did not have casemates, was much thicker, and was backed up by an earth fill. Defending cannon and mortars on the terreplein could fire across the moat and glacis toward any enemy force advancing from the east.[147]

The two bastions at either end of the east front were much more massive in plan than the other three. They had casemated guns for enfilading fire but did not have casemates in the faces. However, their greater area allowed the placement of more barbette guns. Each of these bastions had a powder magazine, and each had three mine chambers which were large enough to contain 1000 pounds of powder in each chamber. They were designed to be selectively exploded should an assaulting force drive the defenders from the bastion. This was supposed to clear the area of attackers and permit the defenders to regroup or reoccupy the bastion.

Further protection from assault was provided by a large gallery at the outer end of each bonnet. From here riflemen could fire on assaulting soldiers crossing the moat or attempting to scale the east front wall.

The north and south fronts of Pickens were each about 155 yards long with the entrance (sally port) in the north front. These fronts were casemated structures. They intersected with the two channel fronts at almost a ninety degree angle, and here somewhat smaller bastions were located. In addition to casemates for enfilading and frontal fire, these bastions each had a cistern for fresh water storage.

The two channel fronts were each approximately 180 yards long. Where they intersected was a somewhat taller bastion called the Tower Bastion. The channel fronts and the Tower Bastion presented a length of over 360 yards facing the channel. Since the casemates of these fronts were designed for two cannon in each, almost half of the armament of the fort faced toward the channel.[148]

The fort as it appears today is not as originally built. The moat has been considerably filled in with sand, and the massive counterscarp on the east side is eroded. Also a fire and explosion in 1899 completely destroyed the bastion at the intersection of the north and channel fronts leaving a large gap in the north side of the structure.

This five-sided, originally five-bastioned fort was of brick masonry construction using a soft burned plain brick, most of which were manufactured in brick yards located on nearby bays and brought to the island by boat or barge. Fort Pickens required approximately 21,500,000 bricks.[149] Granite was used in stairs, main entrances, cordons, and gun mounts. The interior passages and casemates were roofed with brick barrel arches, and where galleries intersected, good alignment was achieved by careful shaping of individual bricks. The mortar joints throughout were thin and straight, demonstrating expert workmanship and care.

The tops of the brick arches were covered with sheet lead, which in turn was covered with packed sand forming the terreplein on which the barbette gun platforms were placed. In time the sheet lead cracked or corroded, allowing water to leak into the casemates below. This was later corrected somewhat by paving the terreplein with two courses of brick and waterproofing the joints with tar.[150]

It was planned that the garrison would be housed within the fort, using some of the casemates for quarters and storage. The peace time garrison was set at fifty, 600 in war, and 1200 when under siege.

The parade of Fort Pickens, which was originally about eight acres in size, was covered with crushed shells; and during the Civil War the shells were in turn covered with pine straw to reduce the glare. In the parade were hot shot furnaces, additional troop quarters, stores and supplies that could remain outdoors, and areas for drill, recreation and training.[151]

Armament for this fort was to be 200 guns, the major part originally 24- and 32-pounders, plus mortars and carronades. However, in 1839, an Ordnance Board recommended an increase in the number of guns to 217, sixty-three of which were to be 42-pounders. At the end of Major Chase's tour of duty at Pensacola, it was reported that 179 guns had been mounted, including ten of the new 8-inch columbiads.

In 1855, another board recommended that even larger guns be emplaced in the nation's forts. This became necessary because European nations had replaced their warships carrying 18- and 24-pounder guns with those armed with 42- and 68-pounders. More and more of the warships were also being powered with steam, and screw propellers were replacing side-wheel paddles, making them more maneuverable.[152]

This new recommendation provided for Fort Pickens to have a total of 221 guns, including forty-two 8-inch columbiads and four 10-inch columbiads. Since these heavier guns would require new platforms and pintles, months were to elapse before the modifications were made. As it turned out, the events of early 1861 found the fort in a run-down condition and few of the guns on hand in position for firing.[153]

Aerial view of Fort Pickens about 1970, before restoration by the National Park Service. Battery Pensacola is in the center, on the original parade ground. Photo courtesy Gulf Islands National Seashore.

Fort Pickens: The War Years, 1861-1865

In January, 1861, Lieutenants Slemmer and Gilmen decided Fort Pickens would be the one Pensacola fort they could defend from capture by the Florida State Militia, the island location influencing their thinking. Pickens, however, had not been garrisoned for almost ten years and was badly run down. Slemmer later reported that they found only forty of the cannon were in position, and fifty-seven of the casemates were unarmed. On these the embrasures were covered with common wooden shutters which would be a scant obstacle to an attacker. After four weeks of hard work, his little command of fifty-seven soldiers and thirty-one seamen had succeeded in putting fourteen more cannon in position.[154]

Reinforcements sent by ship landed in April, and the Union build-up of the defenses on Santa Rosa Island began. That fall it was reported that the Union troops, who were commanded by Colonel Harvey Brown, numbered about 2000, and were opposed by 7000 men under General Braxton Bragg on the mainland.[155]

By the end of summer, five timber and sand bag batteries had been built in the vicinity of the fort. In the fort itself, the Union engineers had the problem of basically reversing the fort's defenses, since it had been designed to defeat a fleet attempting to force its way into Pensacola Bay, supported by a column operating from the east on the island. Now, however, the threat was from the mainland on the north, which side of the fort was designed for lighter armament and contained two of the three powder magazines.[156]

The Battle of Santa Rosa Island was a gauntlet thrown down by the South that had to be picked up by the North. The result was the bombardment of November 22 and 23, 1861.[157] In this fight the Union forces employed fifty-one cannon ranging in caliber to 10-inch columbiads and 13-inch mortars, supplemented by the 24- and 32-pounders of the Federal warships *Niagara* and *Richmond*. In the two day battle the Union guns fired about 5000 rounds to the Confederate's 1000.[158]

Damage to Fort Pickens, compared to that sustained by McRee, was relatively light. Casualties were reported as: Confederate, seven killed and thirty-three wounded; the Union side: two killed and thirteen wounded.

A second bombardment followed on January 1, 1862, and again the damage sustained by Fort Pickens was not severe.

When the Southern forces left Pensacola, in May, 1862, the Union moved the bulk of the troops on Santa Rosa Island to the mainland. For the rest of the war Fort Pickens was garrisoned by an artillery company and a succession of volunteer infantry companies. These soldiers, in addition to manning the fort and providing fatigue parties, were also called on for guard details. The guard was responsible for the prisoners confined in the casemates, for the fort was used as a prison for Southern military and political prisoners, as well as a disciplinary barracks.[160]

An account of the life of a Southern political prisoner at Fort Pickens is given in a booklet entitled, **Kiss the Children for Father, Letters from a Prisoner at Fort Pickens**, compiled by Merritt L. Nickinson. When the war began, Lucious Manlius Merritt, a businessman of Pensacola, sent his family to Alabama, and he remained in the town. When the Union took over Pensacola, the few men who remained were required to sign an oath of allegiance to the United States or face imprisonment. Merritt refused to do so and was confined at Pickens from November, 1862, until released in January, 1863.

After the war ended, Pickens was garrisoned until 1867. A list of buildings on Santa Rosa Island at this time included a two-hundred-foot-long storehouse, an eighty-foot long hospital building, a commissary building, stables, carpenter shop, blacksmith shop, three storage sheds in the fort's moat and a thirty-foot-long wharf. All of the buildings were one story frame structures.[161]

Left unmanned, Fort Pickens became once again the responsibility of the Engineer Corps for maintenance and new construction. The arms and accouterments were looked after by an ordnance sergeant permanently assigned using fatigue details sent to the island from the post on the mainland.[162]

Evening Parade at Fort Pickens by Federal troops occupying the Santa Rosa Island fortification in 1861. Harper's Weekly, May 25, 1861/Pensacola Historical Society Collections.

Fort Pickens: The Later Years, 1866-1980

The next twenty-five years in the life of Fort Pickens was a period of relative inactivity. Troops from the Post of Barrancas came to the island at intervals for training exercises, or when temporary camps were established during the "sickly season." The permanent garrison on the island consisted of a "fort-keeper" with other occupants being employees of the contractors working under the direction of the Engineer Corps. Maintenance was continued at a low level but did not keep up with the damage done by the elements.

Some design and preparatory work was accomplished for mounting larger cannon in the fort. A 15-inch Rodman, weighing 49,000 pounds, was mounted on the Tower Bastion, and was test fired in November, 1868. The guns of the exterior batteries which had been emplaced during the Civil War were removed and some of these were installed in the fort.[163]

A crisis involving Spanish Cuba in 1873 caused a flurry of rearming activity, but the work was stopped within a few months when the crisis was resolved.[164]

Pensacola and Fort Pickens received national attention when in October, 1886, fifteen Apache men, including the notorious medicine man Geronimo, were confined at Fort Pickens. Later the wives and children, numbering thirty-three, arrived. The Indians quickly became a tourist attraction and hundreds of visitors crossed the Bay and trudged through the sand to the fort in order to see the "savage redmen." The excitement subsided when, in May, 1888, the Indians were moved to Alabama. During the stay of the Apaches at Pickens the garrison remained in station through the months protecting the citizens of Pensacola from the "dangerous prisoners."[165]

As the nineteenth century was drawing to a close Fort Pickens, massive but no longer formidable, sat quietly on the sandy shore beside the blue waters of the Gulf. However, change was in the air and the report of the Endicott Board initiated a major program for rebuilding the seacoast defenses on Santa Rosa Island. Included in the recommendations of the board were submarine mines and floating booms to be located at the entrance to the Bay, the mines and booms being defended by rapid fire guns.

Submarine defenses required that the mines and the miles of electrical cables be stored ashore near to where they would be "planted" in time of war. In 1893-95 casemates in the northeast bastion of Fort Pickens were converted into a "mining casemate" and a battery storage room. A cable gallery, a concrete lined and covered trench, was constructed from there to the water's edge. In 1898, at the onset of the

Spanish-American War, two heavy floating booms were positioned at the channel entrance with a 1000 foot opening between them and two lines of submarine mines were placed in the channel. Searchlights were mounted to sweep the channel at night.[166]

Construction was also begun in 1898 on the reinforced concrete platforms for Battery Pensacola located in the center of the parade of Fort Pickens. This modern battery was armed in 1899 with two 12-inch seacoast cannon mounted on disappearing carriages. These guns were capable of hurling an armor-piercing projectile weighing one thousand pounds a distance of eight miles. When they were test fired in 1901 the concussion must have reverberated through the casements of the old fort and startled the ghosts of the gunners of 1861.[167]

An explosion of a different sort took place on June 20, 1899. Shortly after midnight a fire was discovered in one of the casemates just west of the sally port where block and tackle for moving guns were kept with other ordnance stores. A work detail of soldiers on the island formed a bucket bridge, but could not control the fire which slowly burned toward the northwest bastion where 8,000 pounds of powder were stored. The powder exploded at 5:20 a.m. with a roar that was heard for miles around. The Navy Yard sent a tug with hose and a detachment of marines, and after several more hours of hard work, the fire was put out. One man was killed by the flying debris, the bastion was destroyed, and the adjourning casemates were badly damaged. The damage to the fort was never repairs; instead a concrete road was built through the gap to make it easier to get to Battery Pensacola.[168]

The structure of the old fort continued to be used as a storehouse and for machine shops until after World War II had ended. It was then declared surplus and the old guns and other equipment were removed for salvage. The fort was placed under the jurisdiction of the Florida Board of Parks and Historic Memorials in November, 1949, and in 1971, was transferred to the National Park Service as a part of the Gulf Islands National Seashore.

Waterproofing and stabilization work done by the Park Service permitted reopening many areas of the fort that had been closed for safety reasons. Guided tours are conducted throughout the year and the visitor here can see an example of American coastal defense in most of its many phases.

The wooden buildings near Fort Pickens which are now used for offices and visitors' facilities are pre-World War I vintage. They are the surviving structures that were built early in the twentieth century for living quarters, and for offices and shops used during the construction program.[169]

Fort McRee

Name: Fort McRee

Dates: 1837-1906

Location: On Foster's Bank on the western side of the channel entrance into Pensacola Bay.

Built By: United States Corps of Engineers.

Designed By: Chief Engineer Joseph G. Totten. William H. Chase was on-site engineer.

Description: A brick masonry fort of unique design, in plan resembling a broad, stubby airplane wing with rounded ends. Probably the only one of its kind in the United States. The perimeter of the walls measured 360 yards. Vertical height of the walls was thirty-five feet.

Materials Used: Bricks, granite, wood, iron, earth.

Armament: Designed for 128 cannon (including 24- and 32-pounders). The guns were placed in two tiers in the casemates and en barbette.

Garrison: Peacetime, 40; war, 300; under siege, 500.

Cost: $335,000.00

Present Status: Fort McRee was so badly damaged in the Civil War that it was not repaired. The crumbling walls stood until the hurricane of 1906. The location is now under water.

Ruins of Fort McRee on Foster's Bank (Perdido Key) opposite Santa Rosa Island. Photo from the years after the Civil War show damage from Pensacola harbor bombardments in 1861-62. Walls crumbled and finally fell into the Gulf. From Bliss Quarterly, 1897/ Pensacola Historical Society Collections.

Fort McRee, 1837-1906

Fort McRee stood on Foster's Bank, a sandy peninsula extending south from the mainland and forming the western side of the channel entrance into Pensacola Bay. This fort no longer exists, and the site is now under water. It was named for Lieutenant Colonel William McRee, U.S. Army Corps of Engineers.[170] The design which was unique for American forts of this period was required because of the narrow neck of land on which it stood and to permit facing a major part of its cannon toward the entrance channel. In plan, the fort resembled a large, stubby airplane wing, 450 feet long, 150 feet wide, with rounded ends. It had two tiers of guns in the casemates and barbette guns on the terreplein over the casemates. The casemates that did not have guns were to be used for troop quarters, storage, and magazines.[171]

The natural ground on which the fort stood was level with the low tide mark and filling was required to raise the level of the parade to five feet above mean low tide. (Three feet above the mean high tide mark.)

The top of the vertical wall was thirty-five feet above low tide placing the barbette gun platform at thirty feet. The terreplein was twenty-two feet wide all around the fort. The parade was 400 feet long and eighty-four feet wide, and contained two hot-shot furnaces.

The casemates were twenty-one feet tall to the crest of the arch and were divided by means of wooden timbers and flooring on which the upper tier of cannon were placed. The lower tier of cannon were on the casemate floor, six inches above the level of the parade.

The wall of the fort facing the channel was 366 feet long. The entire fort was completely surrounded by a shallow ditch sixty feet wide, beyond which was a low glacis about three feet high.

McRee was to be armed with 128 guns, eighty-two in the casemates and forty-six en barbette. The peacetime garrison was to be forty, in time of war, 300, and when under siege, 500 soldiers. With Pickens it presented a formidable obstacle to a fleet attempting to sail into Pensacola Bay.[172]

It is unfortunate that this fort no longer stands because it had several unique features in its design. Built of brick masonry (the same as the other forts), it presented some problems for the masons. The circular ends with the barrel arch construction of the casemates must have taken many hours of painstaking labor, judging by the quality of workmanship displayed in the existing forts. Plans on file at the Pensacola Historical Museum show a circular staircase at the center of the front. Built as a separate structure and attached to the inner wall, it must have been an impressive display of the masons' skill. Presumably the treads of this and other interior stairs were of granite. Iron stairs and landings were attached to the inside wall near each

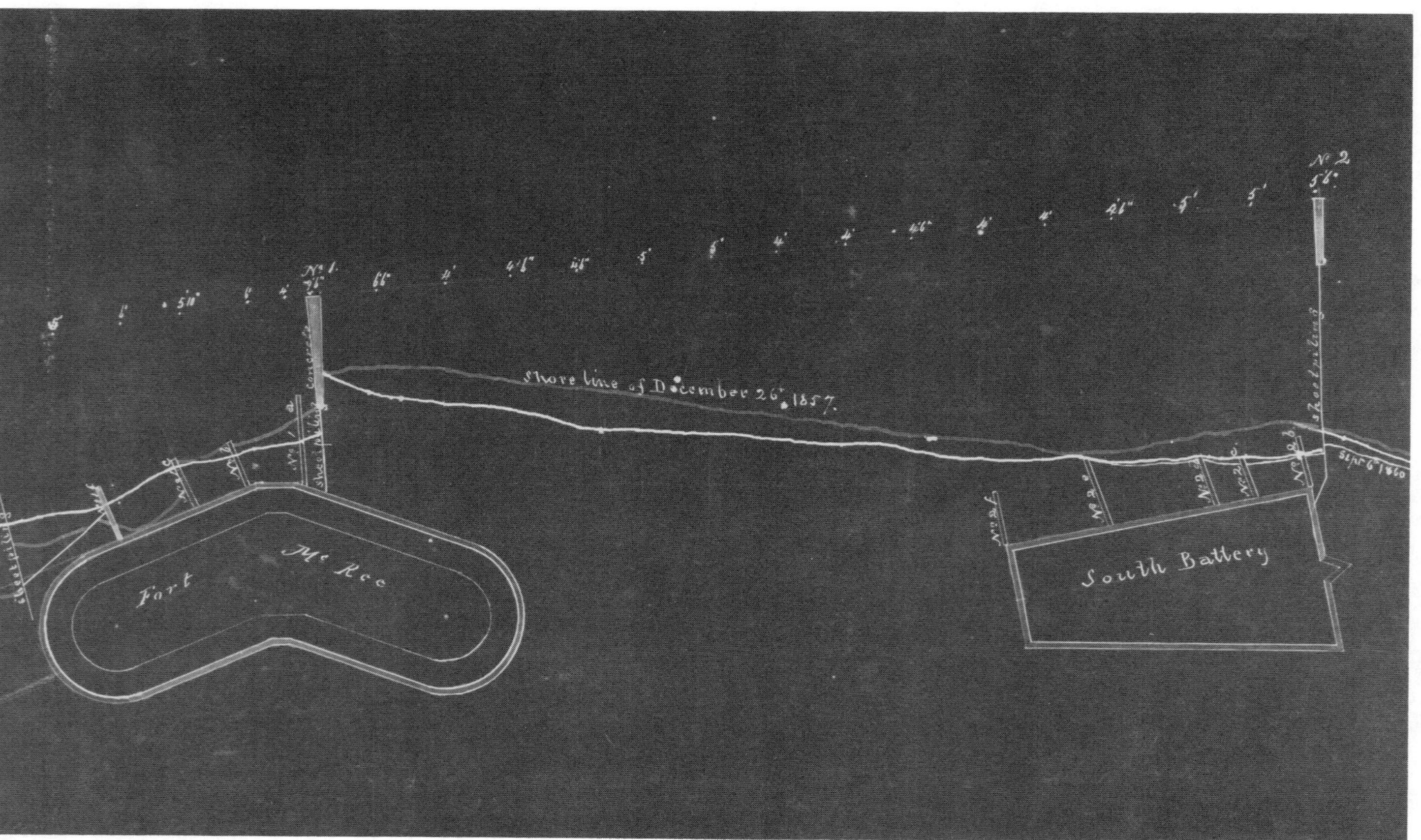

Plan for Fort McRee and the South Battery in 1860. When the Confederates occupied Fort McRee, they renamed the South Battery the Water Battery. Both were damaged in bombardments of November, 1861, and January, 1862. Photo courtesy of National Archives and Record Services, Record Group 77, Civil Works Map File.

end, and led from the parade to the upper and barbette gun tiers.[173]

A letter from a Confederate soldier stationed at Pensacola in 1861 said that one of his comrades was badly injured in a fall down the stairs at Fort McRee. One wonders if the accident occurred on the circular staircase or on the "fire escape" resembling stairs at either end of the parade.[174]

In addition to the circular stair well, two more circular structures are shown attached to the inner wall near each end of the parade. Forming a circular room about eight feet in diamater and fourteen feet high, one can speculate they might have been above ground water cisterns, but the drawings available are not clear about this.[175]

This fort seems to have had considerably more wood incorporated into its design than the other forts that were built at this time. As mentioned earlier, the upper tier of guns in the casemates were placed on lumber and timber platforms. Old photographs on display at the Pensacola Historical Museum indicate that some of the casemates opened into the Parade and the open ends were closed with a framed wooden wall. This may be one reason that this fort was so severely damaged and the guns of the fort stopped answering the Union broadsides in the bombardments of 1861-62. Fires broke out several times and were only extinguished by the heroic work of the defenders.[176]

Fort McRee took three years to build, was completed in 1840, and required 15,000,000 brick.[177] As with Pickens, it was garrisoned intermittently until about 1850, when the first barracks were completed at Barrancas Barracks. After that, the permanent occupants were one or more ordnance sergeants and their families except when troops were sent there for training, construction or maintenance.[178]

Drawings of the site of the fort also show a water-level battery located about 600 yards south of McRee and indicate that this too was a brick structure.[179] In the shape of a trapezoid, 280 feet facing the channel and about 120 feet deep, it was positioned close to the water's edge with the foundations protected from wave action by a number of jetties built out from the shore. Records are not clear on the number of guns to be mounted in this open battery.

Sketches of Confederate gun positions of 1861 show a "Water Battery" in this same location. This battery was badly damaged in the Union bombardments.[180]

At the time it was taken over by the Florida State Militia in January, 1861, there were 125 sea-coast and garrison cannon at the fort, not all of which had been mounted. The departing Federals had taken all of the ammunition they could and had destroyed the rest. The cannon bearing on the channel had been spiked. The Confederate forces repaired the damage and mounted additional guns in both the fort and adjacent battery.[181]

Before the Union commander would begin his planned bombardment of the Confederate batteries, he requested and finally received an assignment of two warships, the *Niagara* and the *Richmond*, to supplement the fire of his cannon on Santa Rosa Island. They became available in November and the firing started on November 22 and lasted through the twenty-third. The ships were able to move close in shore to a position where they could more effectively fire broadsides against the fort.[182] In the ensuing fight both McRee and the Water Battery were severly damaged with McRee being set afire several times. After the first day's fighting some of Bragg's staff recommended that McRee be abandoned and blown-up, but Bragg decided that this would hurt the morale of his troops and ordered that repairs be made as rapidly as possible.[183]

Adverse winds prevented the ships from being as effective on November 23 but McRee had been sorely punished. The January 1, 1862, bombardment was not as damaging to McRee, but in May, 1862, when the Confederates left Pensacola, they set fire to the fort, destroying many of the gun platforms and further weakening the masonry.[184]

The Union forces, on moving back to the mainland, put some troops on Foster's Bank, but as far as is known did not spend any effort on repairs. A Union captain, in a letter datelined Pensacola, February 21, 1863, stated, "Fort McRee [sic] was virtually riddled. There is nothing left of it but the bare walls, and they can hardly stand alone, having been so thoroughly perforated." . . . "Fort McRee [sic] is so far gone, that it is not safe to occupy."[185]

Because it was part of the government reservation, caretakers continued to live on Foster's Bank in the post-war years. However, the once-proud fort was allowed to waste away. In the Winter of 1875-76, working parties of the 5th U.S. Artillery, salvaged brick from the structures at Barrancas Barracks.[186] In Fiscal Year 1878, the account for "Protection, Preservation and Repair of Fortifications" was allocated the following sums:[187]

Fort McRee	$200.00
Fort Pickens	990.00
Fort Barrancas	-0-
Advanced Redoubt	-0-

By 1885, the War Department had constructed additional jetties for the preservation of the shoreline at the site of Fort McRee.[188] This was to preserve Foster's Bank as a location for other harbor defenses, and not to protect Fort McRee itself as in June, 1893, a report by a board studying the defenses at Pensacola reported, "Fort McRee on Foster's Bank was in ruins, most of its fabric having been undermined by the sea and distributed along the shore by the waves."[189]

The hurricane of September, 1906, finished off tired, old Fort McRee. The tide rose twelve feet above normal and gusts up to one hundred miles per hour beat against the walls. When the waters subsided all but a part of one wall was down.[190] In later years some of the brick rubble was used as fill behind the retaining walls built to protect the foundations of Battery Center on Foster's Bank.[191]

What remained of Foster's Bank, now known as Perdido Key, continued to be utilized in the defense of Pensacola Bay. The Endicott System gun emplacements that were built there beginning in the 1890s can still be seen.[192]

Fort Barrancas, 1839-1980

Fort Barrancas was an integral part of the defense plan for Pensacola Bay worked out by the Bernard Board in the 1820s.[193] The final plan of the fort was probably the design of Chief Engineer Joseph G. Totten.[194] Captain W.H. Chase was the on-site architect and engineer.[195] Laborers began preparing the site in 1839 but actual construction was not begun until 1840. Fort Barrancas was completed in 1844. An estimated 6,000,000 bricks were used in its construction. The cost has been estimated as low as $200,000 and as high as $334,000.[196]

The planning of the fort at the crest of the bluffs presented some challenging problems, for the design had to cover several contingencies. Heavy cannon were needed to protect the bay to the south as part of the Pickens-McRee-Barrancas strategy. The fort itself had to be protected from a frontal attack. Lastly, the works had to be defended from a land attack from the rear.[197] The first problem was solved by placing the large cannon on the inner terreplein. Then, rifle ports were included on all four walls to protect against both a frontal and a rear attack. This protection was strengthened by the repairing and modernizing of Battery San Antonio, situated just below the fort, and later by the erection of the Advanced Redoubt to the north.

Fort Barrancas today looks very much like the original construction. It is an irregular polygon,[198] with the forward projection facing south towards the Bay of Pensacola. It has a sally port entrance on the north and dry moats on the northeast and northwest sides. Its overall dimensions are approximately 300 by 300 feet.[199] "The ditch which [parallels] two sides of the main body and the exposed faces of the enceinte overlooking the Spanish battery [is] flanked in each direction by cannons located in the casemates behind the counterscarp wall. Continuous counterscarp galleries connecting these chambers and scarp galleries along the enceinte [contain] closely spaced rifle ports. Like the casemates, both [are] vaulted. Since the fort [is] situated on a rather steep hill, it was impossible and unnecessary to build a counterscarp on two of its sides."[200]

The main work of the fort consists of a perpendicular scarp, capped with a brick parapet. There is an earth fill between the parapet and the wall. Beneath the fill are the casemates and galleries. "The outer works are the features that makes the fort truly unique. Along the exterior of the two inner polygon walls and across the fire moat are the counterscarp walls. Should an invader enter from the rear he would be faced with fire from the two rear walls of the inner fort. Should he successfully weather that, he would have to take the fire moat to gain access to the fort. Once [in] the fire moat, he would be subjected to fire from either side as well as from the two cannon mounted in the intersection of the two counterscarp walls and commanding the moat."[201]

This fire moat, or dry moat, is spanned on the northeast side by a drawbridge which extends from the outer works to the main works and terminates at the sally port. Casemates and galleries with embrasures open into the moat. Casemates are, in fact, located throughout the entire works and face in every direction. They are vaulted rooms, of brick and mortar construction, and are equipped with gun mounts, vertical air shafts for ventilation, and embrasures of various sizes. Two powder magazines are situated in the galleries.

The sally port is a brick-arched and vaulted structure with a granite sill, and it enters the fort below the parade level. Located on the parade are three gun ramps. Here, too, were located in the early years of the fort, a flagpole, a well, and a hot shot furnace.[202] Such furnaces heated solid iron cannon balls to fire at wooden ships.

A subterranean tunnel provides communication between the casemates and rooms of the main works and those in the counterscarp across the moat. Other underground passages and stairs lead to the Battery San Antonio.[203]

Fort Barrancas was constructed to house thirty-three barbette guns and eight flanking howitzers. In 1861, at the outbreak of the Civil War, the armaments credited to the fort were: thirteen 8-inch columbiads and howitzers; two 10-inch mortars; and twenty-four smaller caliber cannons. Some of these guns were moved to Fort Pickens and others spiked when the Federal troops abandoned Fort Barrancas. As soon as the Confederate Army took command of the fort, they began to strengthen its defenses by adding auxiliary batteries along the coast. Thirteen sand batteries (authorities differ on the exact number) were emplaced by the troops, and five major installations were made at the Navy Yard, Warrington Church, Barrancas Barracks, the Old Lighthouse, and the New Lighthouse. The battery at the church was rated the most effective of these. Its fire was both powerful and accurate.[204]

As the Confederates arrived they were settled in temporary camps north of the fort itself. They had no standard equipment or uniforms. When the Alabamians took over the Navy Yard, they found a large supply of United States Marine uniforms which they parcelled out among themselves, one regiment taking trousers, another caps, and so on.[205] The troops spent their days drilling, standing guard, and building the auxiliary batteries along the coast. One soldier reported proudly, but not necessarily accurately, that a mortar used at Fort Sumter had been mounted at one of the sand batteries.[206] Rations were adequate, but sand fleas and mosquitoes were constant torments.

The Confederates' spirits were kept high, in those first months of the war, by reports of the early successes of the Southern armies. A Federal soldier stationed at Fort Pickens relates in his memoirs a story about the Southern troops sailing two small boats from the Barrancas to Santa Rosa Island. These boats had been filled with letters and papers "which narrated in glowing colors MacDowell's utter route...and the impending triumph of the Confederacy."[207]

The elation did not last long. The heat of the summer drastically increased the numbers of cases of typhoid fever and measles in the camp. Hospital care was poor, and the death toll mounted rapidly.[208] By the spring of 1862, southern armies elsewhere were needing men and materials, and the troops at Fort Barrancas were moved to other localities.

The Federal troops moved in immediately, glad to be away from the narrow confines of Santa Rosa Island, glad to trade sand for green grass. Their contacts with the civilian population of Warrington and Pensacola were far different from those of the Confederate army. The Confederates could enjoy dining in town or receiving visits from their friends who came to the fort.[209] The Federals, however, were not welcomed by the citizens, and probably for good reason. All Southern sympathizers who could, had left the area, and those who remained were often looked upon as spies by the Union soldiers. Some were arrested and imprisoned at Fort Pickens. Captain Frank H. Larned reported to his superiors soon after the Federals came to Fort Barrancas that navy men on shore liberty had "wantonly set fire to and destroyed three fine houses" in the nearby village.[210] By summer, things had quieted down, the Union soliders and officers had taken possession of many of the houses left vacant by the departed citizens, and raids and skirmishes were the order of the day.[211] The civilians termed some of these raids "piano raids" because the purpose of the excursions appeared to be the acquisition of furniture for the officers quarters rather than routing the enemy. A Vermont volunteer wrote about one general who, "while in command at Pensacola had discovered a great fondness for pianos and miscellaneous articles of furniture, of which he had a large and interesting collection at his quarters...Subsequently near Port Hudson, this pseudo general was taken prisoner. It was reported that the rebels offered to exchange him for six pianos, but the proposition seems not to have been accepted."[212]

Gradually the soldiers and the civilians learned to accept each other. The citizens were invited to a performance of the Sixth Regiment Zouave Theater when the group presented a program of songs and skits. The performance opened with "My Love, He Is A Zouave" and concluded with a "laughable farce."[213] This group had been organized by the New York Sixth Regiment to ease the tedium of garrison life.

The Civil War period marked the time of greatest military activity at Fort Barrancas. The Confederates had moved in a great deal of armament, but the Union troops, having little fear of attack, kept a minimum of artillery and cannon on the site. After the Civil War a few guns were maintained as part of the coast artillery installations. By 1900 the fort was being used to store powder, cannons, and other equipment for the garrison at the Post of Fort Barrancas. By 1947 all armament had been removed.

Interior brick walls of Fort Barrancas feature arches which support the parapet — where barbette guns were mounted. Photo/Pensacola Historical Society Collections.

Advanced Redoubt

Name:	Advanced Redoubt of Fort Barrancas
Dates:	Construction began in 1845. Continued intermittently until Civil War. Nothing done after 1870.
Location:	Naval Air Station, north of Fort Barrancas.
Built By:	United States Corps of Engineers.
Designed By:	Chief Engineer Joseph G. Totten.
Description:	A trapizoidal fortification, 300 by 330 feet, surrounded by a moat. Faces east and is entered by a drawbridge on the east.
Materials Used:	Brick, earth, metal, and wood. Reinforced by concrete, an innovation in fort building successfully used here.
Armament:	Original design called for eight 24-pounder guns mounted in barbette. 1855 specifications called for eight 24-pounder howitzers in addition.
Garrison:	Four of the casemates served as garrison quarters. Number of troops so assigned not known.
Cost:	Original redoubt: $150,000. Restoration: $600,000.
Present Status:	Restored by National Park Service in 1975-1976. Administered by Gulf Islands National Seashore. Open to the public.

Advanced Redoubt of Fort Barrancas

The Advanced Redoubt of Fort Barrancas was the fourth element (after Forts Pickens, McRee, and Barrancas) in the federal government's plan for the defense of the harbor and the Navy Yard at Pensacola. This plan called for the erection of Fort Barrancas behind the old Spanish Battery San Antonio, and for a line of earthworks north from the new fort cutting across the peninsula towards Bayou Grande. A brick casemated redoubt was to be constructed 1500 yards from Fort Barrancas to anchor the north end of the line.[214]

Major William H. Chase was the first project engineer. Before work could begin, a railroad, eventually 4,000 feet long, had to be extended from the wharf on the bay to the site of the redoubt. Work on the fortification was begun in 1845.[215] The armament for the redoubt, as proposed in the plans of 1843, consisted of eight guns in barbette, which could be converted to embrasured pieces on short notice. Specifications written in 1855 called for eight 24-pounder guns mounted in barbette and eight 24-pounder howitzers mounted in casemate. It is doubtful if all these guns were mounted, as the redoubt was never fully completed. Work was practically halted during the Mexican War for lack of funds. Lieutenant John Newton replaced Chase as project engineer in 1854, and shortly thereafter construction was resumed. It was again halted in 1859, and no major new work was done during the Civil War.[216]

Like Fort Barrancas, the Advanced Redoubt was occupied first by Confederate troops, and then, after May, 1862, by the Union Army. It suffered some damage in the bombardments and in the destruction ordered by the withdrawing Confederate units. The Federal troops decided to maintain and fortify the redoubt because of the Southern raiders still in the area, and the ordnance for it was brought from Fort Pickens.[217] The fortification needed constant attention, and as late as November, 1864, an officer reported that the guns were unsafe for the cannoneers and were almost unmanageable.[218] But on the whole, the structure itself was in fair condition at the end of the war.

After the Civil War, official reports mentioned the need for repairs, and although the plans were approved, apparently little was accomplished. The truth of the matter was that the Advanced Redoubt had outlived its usefulness as a fortification. No land attack could be envisioned, and there is no record of any major work on the redoubt in official reports after 1870.

From 1870 until the 1930s the Advanced Redoubt suffered from decay and vandalism. All metal and woodwork was removed. The east face was even used for target practice, and the curtain still shows the pitmarks made by the shells. The area became overgrown; the moat bridge disappeared.[219] There was an attempt made to restore some of the outer walls in the 1930s, but the results of this WPA project were mediocre.[220]

The construction of the Advanced Redoubt is similar in many respects to that of Fort Barrancas, and like the latter fort, it was apparently designed by Chief Engineer Joseph G. Totten.[221] The site chosen had a difficult and complex topography of small hills and low places, and great care was taken to locate the fortification properly.

Trapezoidal in shape, the fort is made of brick and earth, and it measures 330 by 300 feet.[222] The main work is a raised mound, held in place by a masonry system of interconnected sustaining arches, especially engineered to retain the loose sand. These sustaining arches are in two tiers on the north, south, and west sides. The mound supports the terreplein and parapets of the ramparts and the parade ground. It is surrounded by a dry ditch, a covered way and beyond, a glacis. The interior contains galleries and casemates; and the counterscarp, which also contains small arms galleries and casemates, supports the covered way. The fort is entered from the east by means of a drawbridge extending over the ditch (twenty-five to thirty-seven feet wide) from the covered way to the level of the parade. Stairways in the north and southwest corners lead down to the lower story of the main works. Four of the casemates have served as garrison quarters.

The materials used in the construction of the redoubt are interesting. The brick, locally made, is a medium reddish brown, soft and uneven in texture, and porous. Light gray granite is found in some of the exposed areas. The use of concrete in the construction of a masonry fort was an innovation of the project engineers, as it had been rarely employed for such a purpose before 1845. The concrete is utilized below ground in the footings, under the earth fill in covering the brick vaulting, and behind the brick as a core for the walls. There are no architectural embellishments on the fort, but the brick workmanship is of the highest order.[223]

The original cost of the Advanced Redoubt is given as $150,000.[224] The cost of the stabilization and restoration work done in 1975-76 by the National Park Service is estimated at $600,000.[225]

Entrance to the Advanced Redoubt of Barrancas ("Fort Redoubt") in 1962, before restoration by the National Park Service. Library of Congress photo reproduced as postcard/Pensacola Historical Society Collections.

Bird's eye view of the U.S. Army Post of Fort Barrancas in 1912. Photo/Pensacola Historical Society Collections.

The Post of Fort Barrancas

Name: The Post of Fort Barrancas

Dates: 1821 some buildings ceded by Spain to United States. Area developed to house army troops until 1947, when it was transferred to the Navy.

Location: Naval Air Station, north and east of Fort Barrancas.

Built By: U.S. Corps of Engineers or army personnel.

Designed By: Various people.

Description: Consisted of barracks, officers' quarters, storerooms, and workshops.

Materials Used: Brick, masonry, lumber.

Armament: During the Civil War Period there was a battery near the Barrancas Barracks.

Garrison: Numbers varied. It was the home of the First Coast Artillery and the 13th Coast Artillery, Training camp for ROTC, CMTC, and national and state guards units.

Present Status: Control of area passed from the Army to the Navy in 1947. Some of the early buildings are still in use.

Barracks for quartering U.S. Army troops at the post of Fort Barrancas in the 1890s. Photo/Pensacola Historical Society Collections.

The Post of Fort Barrancas

Neither the Spanish nor the English built forts or stockades at the Barrancas that were large enough to house all the troops and the auxiliary services necessary to maintain a garrison. In each case a series of buildings was constructed to the north of the fort, usually in a roughly semi-circular pattern. When the United States acquired Fort San Carlos de Barrancas from Spain in 1821, the army found just such an arrangement there.

Both the fort and the outlying houses and sheds were in disrepair.[226] During Andrew Jackson's brief administration as military governor of Pensacola, he ordered United States regular troops to begin building new barracks on Hospital Hill, 600 yards east of the fort and near a fine spring. In the autumn of 1822, the contingent of American soldiers stationed in the town of Pensacola was moved to the Barrancas because the old barracks on the Plaza had burned, and because the soldiers were quarreling with the civilians.[227]

The Navy took over the administration of this area in 1825. Commodore Lewis Warrington and subsequent commandants made improvements to what became known as the Post of Fort Barrancas, repairing the old buildings and adding new ones. The old Spanish Hospital had to be abandoned in 1830, and the sick were taken to the new Marine Hospital serving the Navy Yard.[228] The new buildings were, for the most part, located to the east of the old Fort San Carlos de Barrancas.[229]

As work on Fort Pickens and the Navy Yard progressed throughout the 1830s, the Post of Fort Barrancas became the home for part of a United States regiment of artillery. In the early 1840s, the new Fort Barrancas was constructed, and its complement of troops was garrisoned at the post. In 1844 the War Department again assumed control of the Army Reserve, which included, at that time, the new fort, the Post of Fort Barrancas, the Battery San Antonio, and the site of the proposed Advanced Redoubt. During these and later decades, the Post of Fort Barrancas provided living quarters for the troops assigned to Forts Pickens and McRee, as well as the nearby Fort Barrancas.[230]

In the late 1840s, the old barracks were declared inadequate, and ground was broken in June of 1847 for new ones.[231] This three-story brick building, known as the Barrancas Barracks, was 186 feet long and thirty-six feet wide. It was admirably situated on the ridge 600 yards east of Fort Barrancas overlooking Pensacola Bay, near the site of the present Building 1500 which houses the Naval Schools of Photography. In addition to sleeping quarters, there were kitchens, offices, and storerooms in the building. The quarters were well lighted and well ventilated, and each room had an open fireplace. Although originally planned for a full regiment, the Barracks houses only four companies of men.[232] It was the largest building on the reservation for many years after it was completed, and it was occupied from August 1851 until the late 1930s.[223]

Behind the Barracks were four two-story buildings which served as quarters for laundresses and married soldiers. The first floor of the fourth building was used as a jail, and the second floor had a billiard room. About the same time the Barracks were constructed, new officers' quarters were erected to the east of the Barracks.[234] All the work done before 1860 was under the direction of the Army Corps of Engineers, and hired slave labor was used extensively.

The history of the Post of Fort Barrancas during the Civil War parallels that of Fort Barrancas. The post became the headquarters of the Confederate troops in the Pensacola area from January, 1861, until May, 1862. During these sixteen months several thousand soldiers, including regiments from Florida, Alabama, Mississippi, Georgia, and Louisiana, were encamped at the post or nearby. A major battery, consisting of four 6-pounder guns and two 12-pound howitzers, was installed by the Confederates in the Barrancas Barracks area.[235] As the Confederate troops withdrew from Pensacola in May, 1862, they were ordered to burn everything on the post,[236] but this scorched earth policy was not entirely successful.[237]

The Federal soldiers moved across the bay from Fort Pickens, and they found many of the buildings still usable. As the war continued and it seemed unlikely that Pensacola would be attacked, most of the Federal troops were removed from the town to the post. Many of the civilians, concerned about this loss of protection from the numerous marauders in the area, followed the army to Barrancas. There, they built for themselves a temporary community called "Shanty Town."[238]

Among the Federal troops stationed at the Post were regiments from Vermont, Connecticut, New York, Illinois, Indiana, Ohio, and Iowa. Most of these regiments arrived during the last years of the war. They, together with a number of independent Negro regiments, also stationed at Barrancas, formed Major General Frederick Steele's expedition to Blakely, Alabama, as part of his campaign against Mobile in April, 1865.[240]

After the Civil War the Post of Fort Barrancas became the garrison for troops that manned the harbor defenses. A national cemetery was created there in 1868.[241] In the 1870s, new officers' quarters were built, this time west of Barrancas Barracks. A few of these 1870 homes are still in use. The old thirty-bed hospital, converted from a barracks during the Civil War, was improved by the addition of a bathroom. In 1874, a new laundry, large enough to accommodate twelve laundresses, was erected. Stables, a bake house, a commissary, and various shops and storehouses completed the post which had at that time a complement of 125 soldiers and six officers.

In the late nineteenth century these men must have considered their years at the Post of Fort Barrancas a fairly good assignment. Among the amenities they enjoyed were reading and billiards rooms in their barracks. The food supply was adequate, augumented by fresh produce from the post garden and fresh fish from the Gulf of Mexico. The beaches served both for recreation and for good personal hygiene. Several times a week the soldiers were marched to the beach after retreat in order to bathe.[242] The villages of Warrington and Woolsey were nearby, and the post yacht made regular trips to Pensacola. A dirt road also ran from the post to Pensacola.[243] These advantages, unfortunately, were offset by the harassment of insects and reptiles, the periodic epidemics of yellow fever, and the annual threat of the hurricane season.

During the next several decades the Post of Fort Barrancas was enlarged by small acquisitions of land from the Naval Reserve, and new barracks and other buildings were constructed.[244] A new hospital was built in 1895, and it was expanded and improved several times. During the Spanish-American War, the post was the headquarters for the Coast Artillery Corps defending Pensacola Bay. It was the permanent home of the First Coast Artillery, and by 1938 it was one of the largest training centers in the South for such units.[245]

The rapid development of air warfare in World War II outmoded many coastal defense systems. The Coast Artillery was abolished as a separate group, and its members were assigned to other branches of the service. The Post of Fort Barrancas was declared obsolete, and in 1947 control of the Army Reservation was transferred to the Department of the Navy. The Navy has continued to use many of the old facilities as part of the Naval Air Station.

Aircraft Carrier USS Lexington *moored at its home port, the U.S. Naval Air Station at Pensacola in the early 1980s. The modern station spreads from the old Navy Yard adjacent to the boat basin.* Postcard/Pensacola Historical Society.

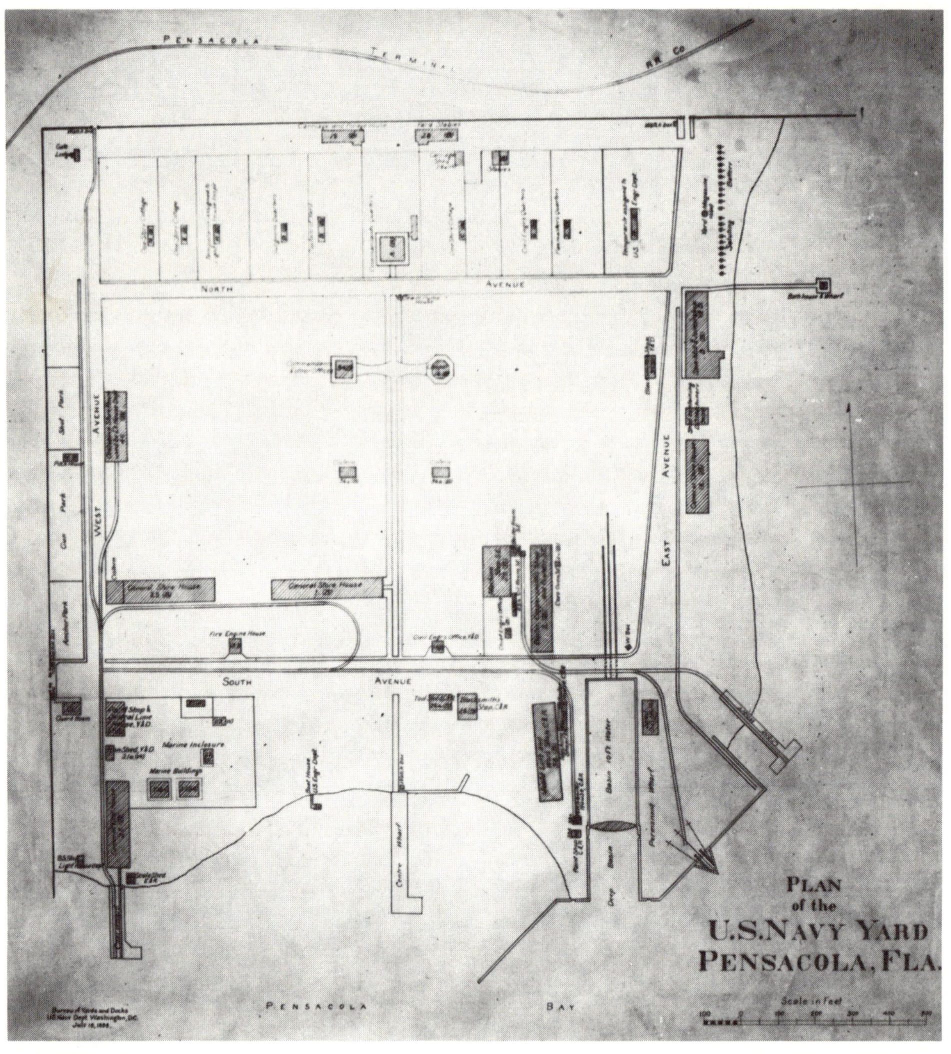

Plan for the Pensacola Navy Yard in 1898. Photo courtesy of the Bureau of Yards and Docks, U.S. Navy.

The Pensacola Navy Yard and Naval Air Station*

Spain transferred Florida to the United States in 1821, and the new lands were given Territorial status by an Act of Congress in 1822. Citizens of the new territory were not slow to adapt to the change of government and began to ask for help from Washington to develop internal improvements in order to facilitiate domestic and foreign commerce.

Communities located on or near the Gulf of Mexico were especially interested in improvements to local harbors, and Pensacola emerged as a strong contender for the location of a Gulf Coast navy yard. Although Pensacola was virtually isolated from the interior and the more populus states, the advantage of its location on the Gulf and its large well-placed bay argued strongly in its favor as the preferred location for a navy yard. On March 3, 1825, the House of Representatives approved a Senate bill authorizing the establishment of a navy yard to be located at Pensacola. On May 24, 1825, the Secretary of the Navy instructed Commodore Lewis Warrington, commander of the West Indies Squadron, patrolling the Gulf of Mexico and the Carribbean, to establish his supply depot at Pensacola, using facilities at Barrancas Barracks that the War Department had agreed to relinquish to the Navy.

In September of that same year, the Secretary sent Captains William Bainbridge and James Biddle to join with Commodore Warrington as a commission to select the site at Pensacola for the new yard. After making an extensive survey of the shore of the Bay, and having made soundings to determine the depth of water at likely sites, the commissioners recommended the yard be located in the vicinity of the Barrancas, and to the northwest and eastward of Tartar Point. In addition to its other advantages, this site already belonged to the United States Government.

President John Quincy Adams approved the selection of the commission in December, 1825, and on February 4, 1826, the *Pensacola Gazette* reported that preparations for the construction of the naval base had begun.

During much of the life of this navy yard, its growth and usefulness was subject to the whims of Congress which were in turn influenced by the domestic and international political climate. A local problem that long plagued the yard was the repeated epidemics of yellow fever which often brought operations to a virtual standstill for weeks or months at a time. Another factor which strongly influenced the size of the appropriations voted for the Pensacola Yard was the fact that Florida as a

* Much of the material for this chapter was taken from George F. Pearce, **The U.S. Navy in Pensacola**. Gainesville: University Presses of Florida, 1980. Numbered footnotes will refer to material from other sources.

Territory had to compete with states which were much more interested in building up the government installations in their boundaries.

In the 1820s and 30s, the Yard grew slowly as the result of limited sums appropriated for its construction. When the war with Mexico started in 1846, the Yard was able to provide very limited service to the ships operating in the Gulf of Mexico. A comparison of expenditures made at three navy yards between 1834 and 1841 shows how the Pensacola Yard compared in size of the appropriations voted:

$723,950. for the Norfolk Yard
668,575. for the Boston Yard
332,100. for the Pensacola Yard

The attitude in Washington changed to some extent about the time that Florida became a state in 1845. In 1848, a contract was let for a floating drydock, basin, and marine railway, and in the 1850s Florida's representatives in Washington succeeded in having the Pensacola Yard selected to build two ships for the navy. Both of these ships were completed as far as the local facilities would permit and were launched in 1859. One of these ships, the U.S.S. *Pensacola*, was to be outfitted with both sail and steam. After it was launched, it was sailed to the Norfolk yard to be fitted with steam equipment and armament, as Pensacola could not handle these jobs.

Even though the Navy Yard had been so long in becoming useful, the expenditures of the Navy Department on the yard, and of the War Department for the construction of the protecting forts had contributed materially to the economy of Pensacola during the years since 1822. As the Yard was about five miles from Pensacola, two villages, Warrington to the west and Woolsey to the north, had been located on government land adjoining the Yard, in order to provide housing for the families of the workmen employed there. Warrington, which was named for the first commandant of the Navy Yard, Commodore Lewis Warrington, became a thriving town with a small business district. Woolsey, named for the second Commandant of the Yard, Melancthon T. Woolsey, remained principally a residential village. Later on, in the nineteenth century, with the advent of railroads and improved public roads, the Yard was connected to Pensacola by a rail line and a road suitable for wagons and carriages.

The outbreak of the Civil War found the Pensacola Yard well equipped for the construction, repair and service of wooden sailing ships, but with limited facilities for repairing steam propelled vessels. Nevertheless, possession of the Yard and its protecting forts became an early objective of the Southern states, even before the Confederacy was formed. As soon as the state legislatures had voted to secede from the Union, the governors of Alabama and Florida sent state troops to Pensacola, and they had no difficulty in taking possession of the Yard and the mainland forts from the small naval and marine guard. The Confederate government used the facilities until they evacuated Pensacola in 1862, at which time they burned many of the buildings and shops as they retreated.

The Federal government made necessary repairs to enable the Yard to service the blockading ships operating in the Gulf of Mexico, but the demands of the War prevented the replacement of the floating drydock and of the machine tools needed in the repair shops.

The end of hostilities and the resulting reduction in the size of the Navy, meant decreased activity at the Yard. Congress, involved in Reconstruction politics, paid little attention to naval affairs, and the future of the Pensacola installation looked bleak. Some of this indecision about the Yard stemmed from the frequent occurence of yellow fever epidemics in Pensacola. As stated before, these usually caused work to stop for long periods until the disease had run its course.

Political patronage enabled the Yard to survive, but the westward expansion of the nation and the increasing industrialization of the North left Pensacola in a backwater. When compared to the navy yards on the east and west coasts, the Pensacola Yard was far removed from the scenes of greatest activity. The Spanish-American War brought a brief spurt of activity, but the acquisition of Guantanamo Bay in Cuba still further eroded the importance of maintaining a yard at Pensacola. In 1911, the Navy Department decided that the expenses of the Yard were greater than its use justified and on October 20, 1911, the Pensacola Yard was placed on a caretaker status.

Even though this sad event occurred other developments were brewing that would being a rebirth of the Navy Yard and a boost to the economy of Pensacola, but who of the persons living and working in Pensacola when the Wright brothers made their historic flight in 1903 would have dreamed of the changes that event would bring to the world?

The United States Navy had become interested in the potential of the "flying machine" as early as 1910. On December 23, 1910, Lieutenant T.G. Ellyson was ordered to report to the Glenn Curtiss Aviation Camp, North Island, San Diego, for flight training, and he became Naval Aviator No. 1. In March, 1911, funds were appropriated for experimental work in the development of aviation for naval purposes. Wright and Curtiss flying machines were ordered, and Lieutenant John Rodgers, who became Naval Aviator No. 2, reported to the Wright Company at Dayton, Ohio, and Lieutenant John H. Towers, soon to become Naval Aviator No. 3, reported to the Curtiss School at Hammondsport, New York, for flying instruction.

The first Navy Aviation camp was set up at Annapolis in the Fall of 1911. Events moved rapidly, more planes were procured, mechanics and ground crews were trained, and in July, 1913 there were fourteen qualified aviators. Later in that year, Navy Secretary Josephus Daniels appointed a Board to draw up a plan for the organization of a Naval Aeronautic Service. When this Board made its report, it recommended that an Aeronautic Center be established in Pensacola. In January, 1914, the aviation unit from Annapolis, consisting of nine officers, twenty-three enlisted men, seven aircraft, with portable hangars and other gear arrived in Pensacola to establish a flying school. Lieutenant John H. Towers, Naval Aviator No. 3, was in charge of the unit, and Lieutenant Commander Henry C. Mustin, Naval Aviator No. 11, commanded the Aeronautic Station.

The months that followed were exciting ones for the personnel involved in the new service. Changes were continually coming from the factories of the pioneer airplane companies, and many kinds of experiments were being tried at the Aeronautic Station. In April, 1915, a flying boat was successfully catapulted from a barge in Pensacola Bay, and a week later, an American altitude record for seaplanes was set at 10,000 feet over Pensacola. Construction activity at the station went steadily ahead and machine shops, hangars, a hospital and numerous barracks were built.

All did not go smoothly, however, as flying these early machines was exceedingly dangerous, and several fatal accidents resulted. In June 1916, Lieutenant R.C. Saufley, Naval Aviator No. 14, on an endurance flight over Santa Rosa Island, was killed in a crash after being in the air for eight hours and fifty-one minutes.

A calamity of another sort struck the station on July 5, 1916, when a hurricane roared in from the Gulf, wrecking planes, wharves, overhead wires, roads, the railroad over Bayou Grande, and damaging buildings. Repairs were made as fast as possible and the work went forward at a rapid pace.

By the end of 1916, about 400 civilians were employed at the station which at that time had a complement of fifty-eight officers, 431 enlisted men, thirty-three seaplanes, one kite balloon, one free balloon, and one non-rigid balloon. At this time the station could train sixty-four student aviators or airmen and sixty-four mechanics in six months. Since the Pensacola station was the only one of its kind, the future was expected to bring continued activity.

The entry of America into the War in Europe meant that the military facilities of the country would need to be rapidly expanded. From April, 1917, through 1918, the expansion of the Pensacola Naval Air Station continued, much of it beyond the boundaries of the old Navy Yard into the villages of Warrington and Woolsey. Woolsey practically ceased to exist as houses were purchased and either demolished or moved to make way for the new facilities. In Warrington, to the west, buildings along a mile of beach were moved to make room for construction of temporary seaplane hangars.

The First Aeronautic Detachment was the first United States military unit sent to Europe in World War I. Composed of seven officers and 122 enlisted men, who had trained at Pensacola, it was commanded by Lieutenant Kenneth Whiting, Naval Aviator No. 16.

At the end of the War there were 438 officers and 5,559 enlisted men at the Pensacola station, which was then one of seven Naval Aviation Stations in the continental United States. Demobilization rapidly reduced the size of the complement at the station and it entered a period of reduced activity. However, the science of aviation as it applied to the Navy continued to bring new developments. In 1921-22, land planes began to arrive at the station to replace the seaplanes used for flight training. This meant that landing fields must be built for the operation of land planes.

Station Field, formerly the blimp field, was enlarged to accommodate land planes. This expansion required that the remaining houses in the town of Woolsey had to be razed.

In December, 1921, the Navy was offered land by the city government for an outlying field. This new field was dedicated on December 7, 1922, and named Corry Field, for W.M. Corry, Jr., Naval Aviator No. 23, the first Floridian to enter the flight training program at Pensacola. This first Corry Field was located in the vicinity of the Booker T. Washington High School on East Texar Drive.

As training in landplanes picked up momentum both Station Field and Corry Field needed to be enlarged. However, land adjacent to Corry Field was not available for lease or purchase. And the county commissioners therefore purchased a 500-acre tract of land west of Pensacola and transferred it to the Navy Department. Here the present Corry Field was built and dedicated in July, 1927. When Station Field was further enlarged in 1936, it was renamed Chevalier Field, for Godfrey de C. Chevalier, Naval Aviator No. 7.

Other events of note occurred at the station during the period between the two World Wars. In early 1920, Charles Lindbergh, while on a barnstorming flight, landed at the air station. His plane needed some repairs which station personnel assisted in expediting. In October, 1927, after his trans-Atlantic flight, while making a cross-country tour, he landed at Pensacola for a short visit as an expression of appreciation for the treatment received on his earlier visit.

In September, 1926, a major hurricane struck Pensacola and heavily damaged the air station. Estimates of the loss ranged to one million dollars, but by 1928 much of the destroyed facilities had been replaced.

The national depression beginning in 1929 was felt at Pensacola, for the air station, like all military installations nationwide, suffered reduced appropriations and program curtailments. However, by 1936, the international situation had brought about increases in appropriations for the military forces. These, and the emergency relief projects of the Works Progress Administration and the Public Works Administration, led to a renewal of construction activity and further expansion.

The need for more space at the Air Station required that two historic landmarks on the reservation be moved. The town of Warrington was relocated across Bayou Grande to the present site in 1930-31. The old Warrington Cemetery, located on the hill overlooking Chevalier Field, was moved to an area adjacent to the Barrancas National Cemetery in 1935.

In 1938, the Naval Air establishment in the Pensacola area consisted of the Air Station and Corry Field surrounded by fifteen auxiliary training and emergency fields located nearby in Alabama and Florida.[246] In 1947, five additional major fields had been built with paved runways, hangars, shops, and facilities for housing and training aviators, supplemented by seventeen auxillary fields.[247]

The end of World War II meant a cut back in the pace of activity at Pensacola, but the era of change continued. Jet powered planes, just emerging in the waning days of the 1940s became a major development of the 1950s, and together with the helicopter, had to be adapted to the needs of Naval Aviation. At the same time training and maintenance facilities had to be altered to accommodate the new technologies.

Hostilities in Korea and later in Vietnam called for an increase in the number of naval aviators to be trained. Finally, missile weapons, together with the entry of the United States into a program of space exploration, found naval aviators training and serving as astronauts and the Naval training facilities adapting to the needs of the space program.[248]

Science and technology had transformed the "art" of flying into a complicated and demanding technical occupation. The result was to bring about a revolution in the methods and equipment necessary to train qualified personnel capable of handling the new "flying machines." The evolution from the crude machines flown by the early aviators, to the space ships manned by astronauts, is described in displays at the Naval Aviation Museum located in the Naval Air Station. Dedicated on April 13, 1975, this museum presents a panorama of the history of Naval Aviation that is educational and inspiring.[249]

One part of the Naval Air Station continues the tradition of the old Navy Yard. The Naval Air Rework facility repairs and services "ships" and "gear" brought to Pensacola from all over the world. The "old salts" of the days of wood and sail would not recognize the present "yard," nor would the pioneer aviators who arrived in Pensacola in January, 1914, when the Navy left the sea and took to the air.[250]

McDonnell 152 — only airplane ever completely built at Pensacola Naval Air Station, photographed in 1916. Photo courtesy Arthur E. Forster.

The Evolution of Coastal Defense Fortifications At Pensacola

Introduction

Much of the material in this book deals with forts and fortifications of the Pensacola area. Therefore, discussion of armaments and the coastal defenses installed at Pensacola and their interrelationship with the defense posture of the United States will be of interest to the reader.

In point of elapsed time, the history of the Pensacola forts can be said to cover a total span of almost 300 years, of which period 123 years represents control by European countries. The remaining time, 160 years of American history, encompasses a much greater effort in terms of materials and man-power devoted to military construction, and the coastal defenses were the major part of this effort.

Little remains of the early installations. Battery San Antonio, the Spanish water battery at the Barrancas, is the major installation of this period that can be seen today. Much remains of the facilities built since 1821. These forts and gun batteries, located on Santa Rosa Island and within the Naval Air Station, are administered by the Gulf Islands National Seashore.

Period from 1559-1821

By the time Christopher Columbus had discovered America, weapons employing gunpowder to hurl a missile were in use in Europe. The explorers and colonists, coming to the New World in the sixteenth and seventeenth centuries, brought with them muzzle-loading hand guns and muskets, on board ships armed with smooth-bore, muzzle-loading cannon. A summary of the important sizes of cannon used by the major European powers at the beginning of the eighteenth century, is given in Table I.[251]

Fortifications constructed to oppose an attacker armed with the siege cannon of this period had to have walls strong enough to withstand a continuous pounding by weapons that could penetrate earthen parapets to the following depths:

Size of shot	Penetration into packed earth
Musket Ball	1½ feet
9 pound ball	6½ to 7 feet
12 pound ball	8½ to 10 feet
18 & 24 pound	11½ to 13 feet

Table I
Important sizes of Cannon in use beginning of 18th Century

Caliber (inches)[1]	Weight of Gun (pounds)	Weight of solid iron shot (pounds)	Designation (See note below)[2]	Maximum Range (yards)
7.0	6000	42	42 Pounder	3500
6.4	5500	32	32 Pounder	2900
5.8-6.0	4800	24-36	24 Pounder	2600
5.2-5.3	4200	18	18 Pounder	2200
4.6-5.0	3000	12-14	12 Pounder	1800
4.0	2500	8-9	9 Pounder	1800
3.6-3.7	1600	6	6 Pounder	1300

1 - The diameter of the bore of the gun was larger than the diameter of the cannon ball. The clearance varied by country and the manufacturer.

2 - When guns fired only solid iron balls the caliber was expressed in terms of the weight of the solid shot.

The early Spanish colonists were faced with many problems in defending their settlements. The most pressing for the early colonists was to ward off attacks by hostile Indians. Consequently the early forts were most likely to be log, or log and earth, stockades and blockhouses which could be built with materials at hand, and gave the necessary protection against the arrows, spears and tomahawks, and, in time, the muskets of the Indians.

Such a stockade would be constructed of logs, fifteen to twenty feet long, eight to twenty inches in diameter, set upright and side by side with the end buried three to four feet into the ground. Secured at the top by horizontal bracing, and further braced by platforms on which the soldiers stood to fire over the top of the palisade, this structure would protect the defenders. If time and manpower were available, the stockade would be further strengthened by building one or more blockhouses two stories high at the corners, or by constructing bastions at various points in the perimeter.

Within the stockade would be the log buildings to house the people, storerooms, and one or more magazines for powder and shot. As the settlement grew the people would move out of the stockade, but in time of danger they would hurry to it and prepare to fight off an attack or to endure a siege.

Defense against an enemy armed with cannon was another problem, for simple log palisades would be quickly smashed by even small cannon, if not opposed by like arms.

The early solution to the problem of defending Pensacola Harbor from an assault by armed vessels was to build a sort of double palisade filled with earth, sand or stone. The earliest forts that were built on Santa Rosa Island and on the mainland at the Barrancas were on this construction, using sand as the fill material. No provision was made in these early fortifications for overhead protection except for the blockhouses and powder storage sheds.

It is beyond the scope of this book to discuss the technical rules for designing forts. However, in order to illustrate the terms used, Figure I is included. It shows the profile of a typical earth fort or redoubt as it might be built by troops using hand tools and manual labor.[253] Depending on the time and the manpower available such defensive works could be as pictured or could be more elaborate and stronger with timber revettments, higher parapets with embrasures, and obstacles placed in the trench and beyond to interfere with the attackers advance.

When the British built Fort George and the two supporting redoubts on Gage Hill (near Lee Square) this basic profile was altered in the fort to include chambers within the parapets to house the soldiers, and brick masonry was apparently used for some of the interior store chambers. However, the cannon were placed to fire over the parapet and the inside of the fort and the redoubts was exposed to Spanish fire from higher ground.

The best preserved of the early fortifications is the Battery San Antonio, built by the Spanish and completed in 1798. It was located on the north shore near the entrance to Pensacola Bay. When constructed it had a thick earth and masonry parapet with open-top embrasures through which the guns were fired, and masonry store chambers in the parade. In 1840 it was modified by the Americans so that the guns were placed to fire over the parapet.

Nothing remains of the other defensive works constructed before 1821. Built of sand and timber, they have fallen prey to the elements and the sites have been obliterated.

1821 to the Present*

When Florida passed to the United States from Spain, the protection of the Gulf Coast harbors came under the aegis of the Federal government in Washington. As early as 1794 the United States had begun to build defenses at the important harbors

* The basic material for this section was taken from Emanuel Raymond Lewis, **Seacoast Fortifications of the United States, An Introductory History.** Washington: Government Printing Office, 1970.

of the Atlantic seaboard. Such activity was to continue, sometimes under great pressure and urgency, at other times in a more deliberate fashion, but virtually continuously until 1947. In fact, building permanent coastal forts was one of the Army's major peacetime activities.

Development of seacoast fortifications was a continually changing process, and the design of a particular fort or set of fortifications depended on a number of interrelated factors that were also changing. Factors to be considered were the weight, range, and power of offensive and defensive armament available at the time, and what was expected to be put to use in the forseeable future. Another factor was the building materials and the techniques to use them, which changed as reinforced concrete came into use. The development of steam-powered, iron-clad ships was a major naval development which had a direct bearing on the planning for coastal defense.

Because the equation was continually being changed the result was a series of solutions or generations of fortifications, based on the best approximation the planners could make at the time. Historians have identified Eight Generations, or periods, of coastal fortifications built by the United States. As Florida did not become a Territory until 1821, it will be classified within six.

The Eight Generations are:

I. Fortifications built during the period, 1794-1804.

During this time the Spanish were rebuilding Fort San Carlos de Barrancas, built Battery San Antonio, and maintained Forts San Miguel and San Bernardo, plus a battery at Punta de Siguenza.

II. Fortifications built during the years 1807-1814.

British and Spanish soldiers were manning the Pensacola forts when General Jackson moved against the town in 1814. The British partially destroyed Fort San Carlos de Barrancas and did destroy the battery at Punta de Siguenza.

III. Permanent fortifications that were built at any time between 1817 and 1867, under the direction of the Bernard Board and the U.S. Corps of Engineers.

This was a period of great activity at Pensacola, during which Forts Pickens, Barrancas, McRee and Redoubt were built.

IV. Fortifications constructed between 1890 and 1910 under a program initiated by the Endicott Board. (Endicott Period)*

Several modern gun batteries were installed in the vicinity of Fort Pickens and on Foster's Bank, near the ruins of Fort McRee. Submarine mine defenses and searchlight batteries were installed during the Spanish-American War. The Coast Artillery Corps was established in 1901 and assumed responsibility for the defense of Pensacola with headquarters at the Post of Fort Barrancas.

V. Fortifications built from 1907 to 1920 as a result of the recommendations of the Taft Board.

Battery Langdon, with two 12-inch guns was constructed in 1917.

VI. Long range, 12- or 16-inch guns were installed in the period 1920-1936.

Pensacola does not have any installations of this period.

VII. Railway artillery was provided at any time in the period between 1919 and 1943.

* The material concerning the Endicott and later defensive works installed at Pensacola is from Edwin C. Bearss, "Historic Structure Report, Fort Pickens and the Endicott Battery," 2 vols., on file at the Gulf Islands National Seashore Library.

Railway artillery was not permanently assigned to Pensacola. In 1922, a 14-inch gun and a 12-inch mortar, each mounted on a specially built railway carriage, were brought to Pensacola for practice firing. The target was the obsolete battleship *Massachusetts* which has been sunk in shallow water in the Gulf with the upper deck and superstructure still above water.[254]

VIII. Fortifications and batteries that were installed between 1937 and 1945.

The two guns of Battery Langdon were put in casemates. Several modern gun batteries were installed.

Table II presents a summary of the installations made at Pensacola during Generations III through VIII, together with data on the types of seacoast artillery of the United States. The following covers some of the details not in the Table.

The three early generations of defensive works built in the United States were for the most part of earth, earth and stone, or earth, brick and stone. All were armed with smooth bore, cast iron, muzzle loading cannon. The Third Generation was of most importance to Pensacola.

In 1816, President James Madison established a board responsible for planning and overseeing the construction of seacoast defenses. This Board was headed by a French military engineer, Simon Bernard, who having served under Napoleon, had come with Lafayette's recommendation to the United States, where he was given a brevet commission as Brigadier General. One member of this board was Brevet Lieutenant Colonel Joseph G. Totten. Totten remained an active member of the board for all of its life, and as the Army's Chief Engineer for twenty-six years, was the man most responsible for some of the impressive harbor defense structures that were produced. Among them are the following forts, made famous by their roles during the Civil War:

Fort Sumter	Charleston Harbor, S.C.
Fort Pickens	Pensacola Harbor, Fla.
Fort Pulaski	Savannah River, Ga.

The Third Generation forts were of brick and stone construction and many are still standing today. These were the first in this country to employ extensively the casemate gun emplacement. This gave additional protection to the guns and crews, and permitted multiple tiers of guns to be installed. These Third Generation forts were armed with smooth-bore, muzzle-loaded guns. Many were placed within a few feet of sea level permitting ricochet fire (skipping the cannon ball on the water), which simplified the gunner's task of aiming the piece.

The years between 1840 and 1861 saw a number of developments which brought cast-iron, smooth-bore ordnance to its peak efficiency. Among these were the cannon called "columbiads," manufactured in 8-inch and 10-inch calibers, firing balls that weighed sixty-four and 125 pounds respectively. A fundamental change in the method of casting the gun greatly increased the strength to withstand the firing pressure, and permitted the production of one piece iron guns in calibers of 15-inches. These were named Rodman guns, for Thomas J. Rodman, an officer in the Army Ordnance Department. Dahlgren and Parrott were names given to other types of guns of new design or method of manufacture. All were used by both sides in the Civil War.

Fifteen-inch smooth-bore Rodman gun at Fort Pickens in 1880. Photo courtesy P.K. Yonge Library, University of Florida.

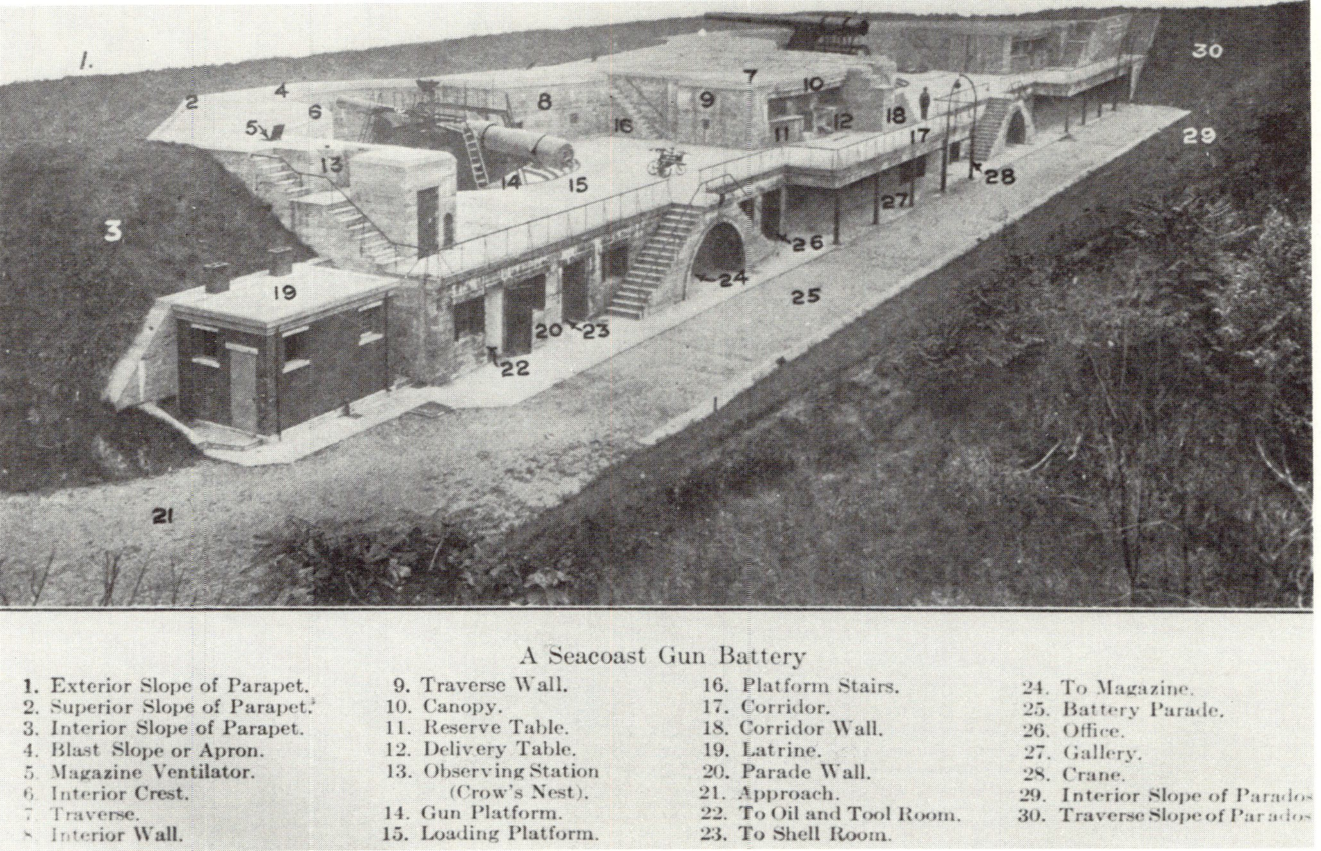

Photo courtesy Gulf Islands National Seashore.

The era of the Third Generation forts came to an end as a result of the Civil War. The improvements in armament and the iron clad ships, both of which were thoroughly tested in the war, rewrote the book on naval tactics and coastal defense. In addition, rifled cannon which had been slowly evolving, were thoroughly tested under war conditions, and had demonstrated the capacity to deliver a heavier projectile at a greater distance with better accuracy than the best smooth bore firing a spherical projectile.

For a period of almost two decades after Appomatox little was done with coastal defense by the United States except to maintain some of the major forts at important harbors. The Pensacola forts received but little attention.

It was well that there was such a pause in expenditures for coastal defense. Several major technical advances revolutionized seacoast armament. These included the use of steel for the manufacture of larger and stronger gun tubes, the perfection of breech loading, and the introduction of more efficient propellants. The cumulative result was that new weapons became available in the last decade of the century that could fire a projectile four times as heavy at effective ranges two to three times as great, with better accuracy.

Nationally, a concern was growing about the country's defense posture, causing President Cleveland to assemble a special board in 1885 to review the entire coastal defense situation and to submit recommendations. This board was headed by the Secretary of War, William C. Endicott.

The major armament of the Endicott Period (1890-1910) consisted of 6-, 8-, 10-, and 12-inch guns, most of which were mounted on the disappearing type carriages. With this carriage, the energy of recoil lowered the gun within the emplacement where it could be serviced and reloaded while remaining concealed from enemy fire. These guns were placed in massive reinforced concrete structures further protected by thick earth embankments or aprons.

A second kind of heavy arm of the Endicott Period was the 12-inch mortar which fired a 700-pound shell in a high arc so that it fell on the lightly armored deck of the opposing ships.

Submarine mine fields were employed to guard the approaches to harbors, and these were protected by smaller caliber (3- to 6-inch) guns that could be loaded and fired rapidly.

Endicott System batteries that were installed on Santa Rosa Island were: Battery Cullum, 10-inch guns; Battery Worth, 12-inch mortars; Battery Van Swearingen, 4.7-inch guns; Battery Pensacola, 12-inch guns; Battery Cooper, 6-inch guns; Battery Payne, 15-pounder guns; Battery Trueman, 15-pounder guns. Installations on Foster's Bank were: Battery Slemmer, 8-inch guns; Battery Center, 15-pounder guns.*

All of the Endicott System has been removed. However, one 6-inch gun mounted on a disappearing carriage has been installed at Battery Cooper as an exhibit.[255]

In 1905, President Theodore Roosevelt convened a group, similar to the Endicott Board, which was headed by Secretary of War William Howard Taft. This new board was to pick up the activity of the previous one by updating and modernizing the

* See alphabetical list of military installations for further details.

defense installations, and to consider the requirements for the new territories acquired as a result of the Spanish-American War.

Battery Langdon was built in 1917, and mounted two modern 12-inch guns. Two of the four guns in Battery Cullum were redesignated as Battery Sevier. Battery Fixed, consisting of two 3-inch anti-aircraft guns was installed. During World War I, both the Army and Navy had Anti-Aircraft guns on Santa Rosa Island.

The period following the First World War (Sixth Generation) found greater emphasis given to dispersion of the defense installations. In the 1930s, Battery Fixed was relocated and modernized. Improved versions of the 155mm gun using the "Panama Mount" were set up on Santa Rosa Island, and designated Battery GPF.

In 1926, the underwater defenses of Pensacola were taken from the Army and assigned to the Navy.

Overlapping in time, and carrying the Sixth Generation concept of dispersion even further, were the installations of the Seventh Generation, which emphasized mobile artillery. Two types were used, one having the guns mounted on railroad cars, the other employing tractor drawn field pieces that could be moved overland and set up on prepared emplacements. Pensacola did not have such installations.

By the middle 1930s, greater emphasis was being placed on protection from bombing from aircraft. Improved anti-aircraft batteries were being put in place, and training of crews was emphasized. In addition the more modern of the fixed-gun emplacements were being put in massive casemates. Battery Langdon was casemated, the walls of the reinforced concrete being about ten feet thick.

Four 90mm anti-motor torpedo boat guns were set up on Santa Rosa Island, two on fixed mounts and two on mobile mounts.

In terms of the gun types, the Eighth Generation were the least varied. The majority of new installations were either of the 16-inch naval gun (twenty-six mile range), or a newly developed 6-inch gun with a fifteen-mile range. Two 6-inch gun batteries were constructed at Pensacola with two guns at each. Battery 233 is located near the site of Fort McRee and Battery 234 is on Santa Rosa Island. The guns were never installed at either battery. In the 1970s the Gulf Islands National Seashore received two of the 6-inch guns from the Smithsonian Institution which were placed at Battery 234 as an exhibit.[256]

The end of World War II brought to a close the era of coastal defenses as the nation's primary shield from a foreign invader.Nuclear explosives and the rocket has made the entire country vulnerable to attack and the narrow coastal shield had lost its usefulness. The Coast Artillery Corps has been disbanded and the personnel transferred.

For 300 years the Pensacola area had seen men toil to build defenses against a real or expected agressor. The physical result of part of this effort has disappeared forever, but much still remains, preserved and maintained for us to see and to study.

Table II
Summary of Generations of the United States Seacoast Fortifications and Typical Armament of the Period (1)

Generation	Period (years)	Fortifications and/or Batteries at Pensacola	TYPICAL USA SEACOAST WEAPONS OF THE PERIOD: Caliber and Type		Gun Weight (pounds)	Solid Projectile Weight (pounds)	Range (yards)
III	1817-1867	Forts Pickens, McRee	24 Pounder	SB	5500	24	1700
			32 Pounder	SB	7500	32	1900
		Barrancas and Redoubt	42 Pounder	SB	8500	42	1900
			10 inch	SB	15400	125	5600
	(1860-1890)		(15 inch	SB	49000	400	6000)
IV (Endicott)	1890-1910	Batteries Cullum, Worth, Slemmer, Pensacola, Van Swearingen, Trueman, Payne, Cooper, Center. Submarine mines and searchlights.	12 inch	RG	116000	1070	13500
			12 inch	RM	29000	700	15200
			6 inch	RG	19000	108	16000

V (Taft)	1907-1920	Battery Langdon, Sevier, Battery Fixed (AA). Submarine mines and searchlights.	14 inch 12 inch	RG RM	138000 33000	1560 700	24000 19300
VI	1917-1936	Battery GPF (155mm) AA Batteries (Panama Mount) 1926 - Navy took over underwater defense at Pensacola.	16 inch 12 inch	RG RG	385000 118000	2340 975	49100 30100
VII (Mobile Artillery)	1919-1943	AMTB Batteries RR guns in Pensacola for practice.	14 inch 8 inch	RG RG	234000 42000	1400 260	48200 35300
VIII	1937-1947	Battery Langdon in casemates. Batteries 233, 234.	16 inch 6 inch	RG RG	307000 22000	2240 105	45100 27000

SB=Smooth Bore; RG=Rifled Gun; RM=Rifled Mortar.

(1) Data on typical seacoast weapons from "Seacoast Fortifications of the United States: An Introductory History," E.R. Lewis.

Profile of a Fortification to Show the Names of the Parts

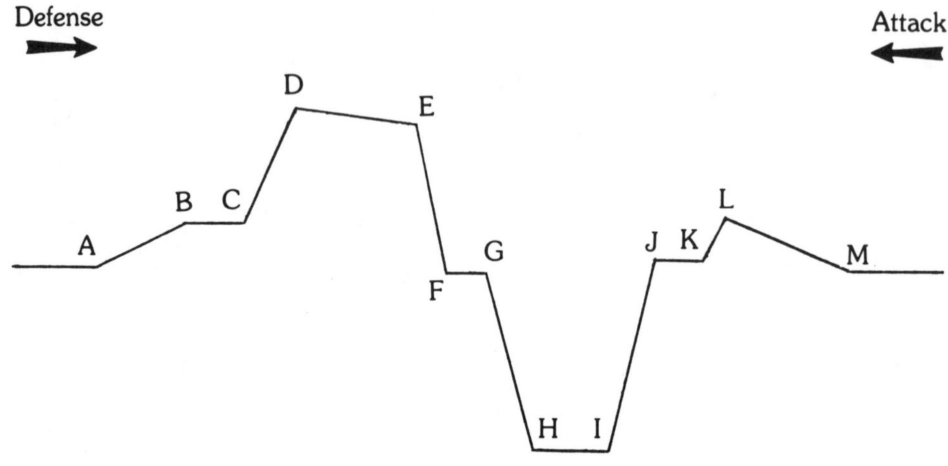

ABCDEF	Profile of the PARAPET
GHIJ	Profile of the DITCH
KLM	profile of the GLACIS
AB	The BANQUETTE slope
BC	TREAD
DE	CREST
FG	BERM
GH	SCARP
IJ	COUNTERSCARP
HI	Bottom of DITCH

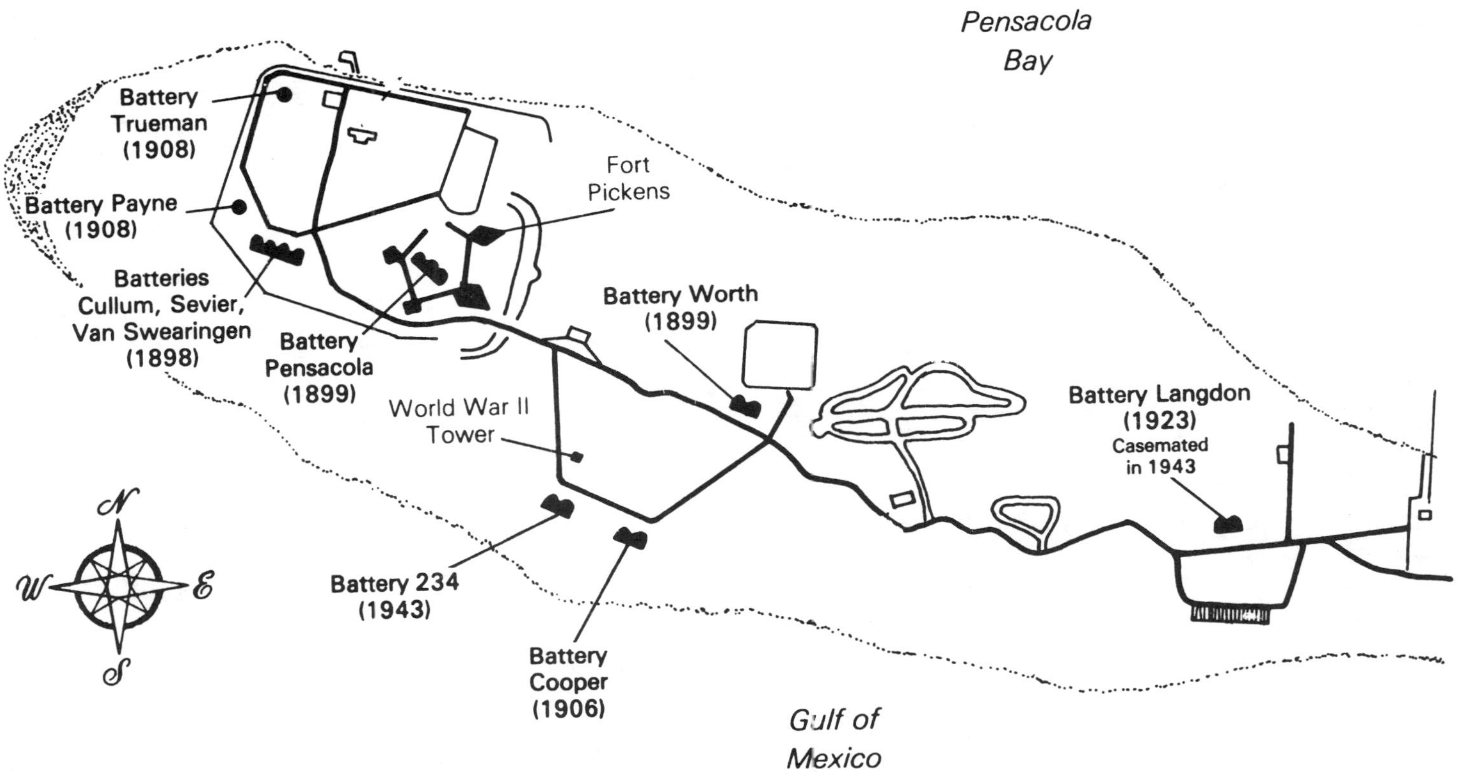

Fort Pickens and surrounding batteries on the western tip of Santa Rosa Island, as maintained in the 1980s by the National Park Service. Map courtesy Gulf Islands National Seashore.

List of Posts, Camps, Stations, Fields, Batteries, and other Military Installations in the Escambia County Area From 1698 to the Present Day

Admiral Mullinnix Field

"The world's smallest airport." Was located at Corry Field. Constructed in 1949 for use by Navy and civilian model airplane builders. The first model plane meet was held at the field on February 20, 1949.

Advanced Redoubt of Fort Barrancas (Fort Redoubt) (Redoubt)

Fortification to the north of Fort Barrancas. One of the four forts built by the United States to protect Pensacola Bay and the Navy Yard.

Advanced Redoubt of Fort at Pensacola (Fort San Miguel)

A redoubt located north of the stockade (Fort San Miguel) on Tarragona Street between today's Romana and Intendencia Streets.

Aguero, Punta de (Tartar Point)

Sand spit within Pensacola Bay, northeast of Fort San Carlos, named in 1693. There was a blockhouse here during the British occupation, which they destroyed when the Spanish landed in March-April, 1781.

Another Redoubt of Fort at Pensacola (Fort San Miguel)

Constructed by the British in 1770s, near a point of land just east of Florida Blanca Street.

Army Reservation (Army Reserve)

Land held by the United States Army, on the north side of Pensacola Bay, west of and adjoining the Navy Yard. Approximately 1700 acres and included the sites of Fort Barrancas, the post of Fort Barrancas, Redoubt, and Battery San Antonio.

Asturias, Fort Principe de

Small Spanish wood and sand fort at Point Siguenza on Santa Rosa Island. Built 1719, destroyed by French troops.

Bagdad Field

Naval Air Station auxiliary field located west of Bagdad, Florida. No longer in use.

Barin Field (in Alabama)

Naval Auxiliary Air Station located near Foley, Alabama. Built 1942. Named in honor of Lt. Louis T. Barin, Naval Aviator No. 56, co-pilot of NC-1 on trans-Atlantic attempt in 1919.

Barrancas Barracks

Term applied to the barracks built to house the U.S. Army troops assigned to the defense of Pensacola during the pre-Civil War period. Later incorporated into the Post of Fort Barrancas.

Barrancas Coloradas (Red Cliffs)
Barranca, La
Barrancas, Las

Various names given by Spanish explorers to the sand bluffs on the north shore of Pensacola Bay opposite the entrance channel from the Gulf of Mexico. This was the site of early Spanish fortifications.

Barrancas Line

In 1863 the Union forces at Barrancas, in order to guard from surprise attack from the west, built a string of earthworks and rifle pits from the Redoubt to Fort Barrancas. In the Winter of 1864-65 this was strengthened and extended. A Redan, embrasured for eight field guns, was built near Bayou Grande on the right flank, and rifle pits were constructed between the Spanish Battery (Barrancas Water Battery) and the beach.

Barrancas National Cemetery

Created in 1868. Located on the Army Reservation, now the Naval Air Station, at the intersection of Hovey and Duncan Roads.

Barrancas Redoubt

The Redoubt was garrisoned in 1862-63 by Company C of the 7th Regiment of Vermont Volunteers. See Advanced Redoubt of Fort Barrancas.

Battery 233

Located near the site of Fort McRee on Foster's Bank. Constructed in 1946. Two 6-inch shield guns. The carriages were received and mounted, but the guns were never installed.

Battery 234 (Brown)

Located on Santa Rosa Island west of Battery Cooper. Constructed in 1946. Two 6-inch shield guns. The carriages were received and mounted, but the guns were never installed. After the Gulf Islands National Seashore Park was established two 6-inch shield guns were installed as an exhibit.

Battery AMTB (Anti Motor Torpedo Boat)

Four 90mm AMTB guns were installed on Santa Rosa Island in 1943. Two were on fixed mounts and were located near Battery Cullum. Two were mobile guns. Removed after World War II ended.

Battery Arriola

Constructed in early 1862 by Confederate troops under General Bragg. Located on Town Point (Gulf Breeze, Florida), it consisted of a single mortar.

Battery Brown

See Battery 234.

Battery Cameron

Installed by Union troops in 1861 on the bay side of Santa Rosa Island, 600 yards northeast of Fort Pickens. Two 10-inch Columbiads. May have been named for Simon Cameron who was Secretary of War in President Lincoln's cabinet, until he was replaced by Edwin M. Stanton in 1862.

Battery Center

Located on Foster's Bank, northeast of Battery Slemmer. Construction started in 1899, completed 1901. Four 15-pounder rapid fire guns. Named in honor of Lt. J.P. Center, Adjutant, 6th U.S. Infantry, killed in the Battle of Okeechobee, 1837. Declared surplus and removed in 1920.

Batteries, Confederate

In 1861 and early in 1982 the Confederate forces under General Bragg built approximately 18 gun emplacements along the northern shore of Pensacola Bay, from Tartar Point (site of Navy Yard) to Fort McRee and established the water battery to the south of Fort McRee. These batteries were constructed of timbers and sand bags. The guns emplaced, which were in addition to those in the forts, were all positioned to fire at Fort Pickens, then held by the Federal troops, and at any ships attempting to enter the Bay. All of these batteries were dismantled and the guns were removed when the Confederate forces evacuated Pensacola in May, 1862.

Undoubtedly, each of these batteries was given an identifying name, but the authors have been able to identify only the following in written accounts:

Marine Battery, near the Wet Slip, NAS
A battery in the Navy Yard
A battery in Warrington village, near the church

Gun Port of Battery Langdon east of Fort Pickens on Santa Rosa Island, as photographed in 1942. Photo by William Z. Harmon/Pensacola Historical Society Collections.

Battery 234 on Santa Rosa Island in the 1970s, as restored by the National Park Service. Constructed in 1946, the battery was designed for two 6-inch shield guns, although the guns were never installed by the U.S. Army. After the establishment of Gulf Islands National Seashore, the guns were mounted as part of the historical interpretation of the Fort Pickens area. Photo courtesy Gulf Islands National Seashore.

Practice firing of seacoast mortars at Battery Worth on Santa Rosa Island in the 1920s. Eight 12-inch mortars originally were installed when the battery was completed in 1899. Photo courtesy of Gulf Islands National Seashore.

A battery near the Barrancas Barracks
A battery near the old Lighthouse site
A battery south of the new Lighthouse
Water battery of Fort McRee
Wheats Battery

Battery Cooper

Located east of Fort Pickens on the south side of the island. Construction started in 1905, completed 1906. Two 6-inch guns mounted on disappearing carriages. Named in honor of Second Lieutenant George A. Cooper, 15th U.S. Infantry, killed in action at Mavitas, Philippine Islands, September 17, 1900. In World War I the guns were removed and sent to Europe for mounting on railway cars. The disappearing carriages were kept until 1920, then declared obsolete and salvaged. After the establishment of the Gulf Islands National Seashore Park, one 6-inch gun mounted on a disappearing carriage has been reinstalled as an exhibit.

Battery Cullum

Located west of Fort Pickens on the south side of the island. Construction started in 1895, completed 1898. Originally four 10-inch guns mounted on disappearing carriages. Named in honor of Brigadier General George W. Cullum. Commissioned as a Second Lieutenant of the Corps of Engineers in 1833, served in the American Civil War and retired in 1874. See Battery Sevier. Guns and carriages removed and salvaged in 1942.

Battery Fixed

A battery of two 3-inch anti-aircraft guns installed in 1917 on Santa Rosa Island about 1,000 yards east of Battery Worth. In the 1930s, this Battery was relocated to a site east of Battery Langdon and newer carriages and guns were installed. It was declared obsolete and dismantled in 1945.

Battery GPF (Grande Puissance Filloux)

In 1934-37 a battery of four 155mm guns (GPF) was installed at Battery Cooper on Santa Rosa Island and designated Battery GPF. The Battery was dismantled in 1945. NOTE: The United States copies the French 155mm (GPF) gun, World War I model. This battery was armed with an improved version, but the designation GPF was retained.

Battery Langdon

Located east of Fort Pickens near the present Ranger Station. Construction started in 1917, completed 1923. Two 12-inch guns mounted on barbette carriages. The battery was named in honor of Brigadier General (Retired) Loomis L. Langdon, who, as a Lieutenant, had served at Fort Pickens from February 1861 to January 1862. Declared surplus in 1947, the guns and carriages were scrapped.

Battery Lincoln

Installed by Union troops in 1861 on a strand of Santa Rosa Island east of Battery Cameron. Two 10-inch siege mortars and four 8-inch seacoast howitzers. Named for President Abraham Lincoln.

Battery at "Old Spanish Fort"

See Old Spanish Fort Battery

Battery Payne

Located on the southwest tip of Santa Rosa Island. Construction started and completed in 1904. Two 3-inch guns mounted on pedestal carriages. Named in honor of Colonel Matthew M. Payne who had entered the service of the United States in 1812, served in the War of 1812, and in the Mexican War. Dismantled in 1946.

Battery Pensacola

Located within Fort Pickens. Construction started in 1898, completed 1899. Two 12-inch guns mounted on disappearing carriages. Battery was declared surplus and the guns were removed in 1934 and carriages removed in 1942.

Battery San Antonio

Built 1797-98 by the Spanish below Fort San Carlos de Barrancas. This was the water battery of the fort. It was enlarged and remodeled by the United States in 1839-44.

Battery Scott

A Union battery located on the tip of Santa Rosa Island, southwest of Fort Pickens.

Battery Sevier

Located adjacent to Batteries Cullum and Van Swearingen. Two 10-inch guns mounted on disappearing carriages which were originally part of Battery Cullum, were redesignated as Battery Sevier. Named in honor of John Sevier, a pioneer, soldier, and first governor of Tennessee. The guns and carriages were removed and salvaged in 1942.

Battery Slemmer

Located on Foster's Bank (site of Fort McRee) to the west of the ruins of that fort. Construction started in 1898, completed 1899. Two 8-inch guns mounted on disappearing carriages. Named in honor of Lieutenant Colonel Adam J. Slemmer, commissioned Second Lieutenant in U.S. Army in 1850. Commanded Union forces at Fort Pickens in 1861, and served at various posts during the Civil War. In 1917 the guns were removed and shipped to Europe for mounting on railroad cars. The carriages were scrapped in 1920.

Battery Totten

A Union battery installed in 1861 on the south side of Santa Rosa Island east of Fort Pickens. One 12-inch and one 13-inch seacoast mortar. Named in honor of Joseph G. Totten, Chief Engineer, Corps of Engineers.

Battery Trueman

Located on the northwest tip of Santa Rosa Island. Construction started and completed in 1905. Two 3-inch guns mounted on pedestal carriages. Named in honor of Major Alexander Trueman, who joined the United States Army in 1790, died of wounds received in action against the Indians near Fort Recovery, Ohio, June, 1792. The battery was dismantled in 1946.

Battery Van Swearingen

Located adjacent to Battery Cullum. Construction started and completed in 1898. Two 4.7-inch guns mounted on pedestal carriages. Named in honor of Joseph Van Swearingen, commissioned a Second Lieutenant in U.S. Army in 1824, served in the Black Hawk War, 1832, killed in action against the Seminole Indians, 1835. The guns and carriages were removed in 1921.

Battery Worth

Located east of Fort Pickens, close to the present road. Construction started in 1897, completed 1899. Eight 12-inch mortars. Named in honor of Brevett Major General William J. Worth, commissioned First Lieutenant in U.S. Army, 1813, served in the Indian Wars and in the Mexican War. In 1918 four mortars were removed. In 1942 Battery was declared obsolete and the guns and carriages were removed for salvage.

Bauer Field

NAS auxiliary field located south of Bronson Field. No longer in use.

Bayou Field

NAS auxiliary field located near the west end of Bayou Grande. No longer in use.

Bell's Field

NAS auxiliary field located west of City Field. No longer in use.

Bluff Springs

See "Camp at Bluff Springs."

Brewton Field (in Alabama)

NAS auxiliary field located south of Brewton, Alabama.

Bronson Field

Naval Auxiliary Air Station, located on Perdido Bay west of Corry Field. Built in 1942. Named in honor of Lieutenant (Junior Grade) Clarance K. Bronson, Naval Aviator No. 15, killed by premature explosion of a bomb during early bomb dropping tests from an airplane, November 8, 1916. Only the runways are still being used.

Brown's Camp (Camp Brown)

A Union troop cantonment on Santa Rosa Island, located about 1½ miles east of Fort Pickens. Occupied by the 6th Regiment New York Volunteers in 1861. Named for Colonel Harvey Brown, commanding officer of the Union troops stationed on Santa Rosa Island.

Camp Alabama

Camp of the 1st Regiment Alabama Volunteers located on the mainland near the village of Warrington. Occupied from about March, 1861 to May, 1862.

Camp Arnold

A Camp established by the 75th New York Infantry (Volunteers) on the mainland near Fort Barrancas in June, 1862, and also occupied by the Maine 15th Regiment Infantry in Fall, 1862.

Camp at Bluff Springs

After the Confederate troops evacuated Pensacola in May, 1862, they established camps of observation at Bluff Springs, Florida, and Pollard, Alabama. Bluff Springs is between U.S. Highway 29 and the Escambia River approximately 30 miles north of Pensacola.

Camp at Florida Point

In 1865 the Union Iowa 20th Regiment camped at Florida Point, which is on the east side of Perdido Pass.

Camp Barrancas

This name was applied in the 1840s and after to the Field Artillery camp for troops assigned to garrison Fort Pickens, McRee, Barrancas and Redoubt. Located on the mainland, east of the site of Fort Barrancas, on land transferred by the Navy to the War Department in May, 1844. The name was used interchangeably with Barrancas Barracks during the period 1840-1870. The name CAMP BARRANCAS was also applied to a temporary camp established in June, 1877, and occupied by the Field Artillery troops from the post on the Barrancas (Camp Barrancas or Barrancas Barracks) to escape yellow fever. This temporary camp was near Sellers Station on the railroad north of Pensacola.

Camp Bennett

Temporary camp established at the NAS in 1918. Located west of the hospital, it housed incoming recruits.

Camp Brady

In 1822, a yellow fever epidemic caused the American Army troops at Fort Barrancas to move to Camp Hope at Galvez Spring. These troops set up a temporary camp which was called Camp Brady. (See Cantonment Clinch)

Camp Bronson

A temporary camp established by the NAS in 1917-18, for aerial bombing practice. Located at Magnolia Point on Escambia Bay.

Camp Brown

See Brown's Camp

Camp Chalmers

Camp of Quitman (Mississippi) light infantry, Confederate forces, in vicinity of Fort Barrancas in late 1861, early 1862.

Camp Coburn

A Union troop camp of the 15th Maine Volunteers on the grounds of the hospital at Fort Barrancas, occupied in 1861.

Camp Davis

A Confederate troop camp located west of Fort Barrancas, occupied 1861-62, probably by Alabama units.

Camp Ferris

Camp of the 28th Regiment, Connecticut Volunteers, located on the mainland about one mile from Fort Barrancas and one-half mile from the Redoubt. Probably named for Colonel Ferris of the 28th Connecticut Regiment.

Camp Galvez Spring

In April, 1823, the American Army troop camps, Camp Brady and Camp Hope, which were both located in the vicinity of Galvez Spring, were combined and redesignated Camp Galvez Spring. (See also Cantonment Clinch) Officially designated Cantonment Clinch on July 4, 1823.

Camp Gonzalez

A Confederate camp (7th Alabama Calvary) on the railroad at Gonzalez, fifteen miles north of Pensacola. It was here, in July, 1864, that Fort Hodgson was built.

Camp Hope (also Camp New Hope)

This was the name given to the camp of American Army troops located at Galvez Spring in 1822. (See Camp Brady and Cantonment Clinch.) Some sources give the name as Camp New Hope.

Camp Jackson

A Union camp on the mainland in vicinity of Fort Barrancas, probably occupied by the 6th new York Infantry (Volunteers) in 1862 after this unit moved from Santa Rosa Island to the mainland.

Camp Lincoln

This was a Union camp on Santa Rosa Island near Fort Pickens housing 6th New York Infantry.

Camp Lomax

This was a Confederate camp for Alabama troops commanded by Colonel Tennant Lomax. It was located on Escambia Bay.

Camp Magnolia

Troop camp of the 9th Regiment, Mississippi Volunteers, in 1861-62. It was located north of the east end of Grande Lagoon and west of Fort Barrancas.

Camp Morgan

Union camp for 91st New York Infantry (Volunteers) probably located in vicinity of Fort Barrancas, 1862 and 1863. In June, 1876, the War Department, as a precautionary measure from yellow fever, moved three companies of the Field Artillery Battalion at the Barrancas to a temporary camp on the north side of Bayou Grande, three miles from the barracks. This bivouac was designated Camp Morgan in honor of the late Brevet Brigadier General C.H. Morgan of the 4th U.S. Artillery. One battery remained at the Barrancas to protect the property. The troops returned to their barracks in the Fall.

Camp Mustin

Temporary camp established at the NAS in 1918. It was located between the hospital and Warrington Beach. It was used as quarters for enlisted men.

Camp New Hope

See Camp Hope.

Camp on Perdido Bay

In the Civil War diary of Dr. Joseph Dill Alison, entries for May, 1861, refer to a Confederate guard camp "on Perdido Bay, a half mile from the Gulf."

Canvas hangars and tents blend with the white sand of Santa Rosa Island at Camp Saufley, established by the U.S. Navy for seaplane training during World War I. Photo/Pensacola Historical Society Collections.

In 1864, Union troops from Barrancas moved to Perdido Bay and found an abandoned Confederate camp on the narrow neck between the Perdido and the Gulf. It may have been the same location as reported by Dr. Alison.

Camp Osceola

In April, 1888, ships of the North Atlantic Squadron, U.S. Navy, visited Pensacola. Approximately 600 sailors and marines from the squadron were encamped at Magnolia Bluff (East Pensacola Heights) on Escambia Bay for several days, and there held parades, drills and maneuvers.

Camp Philips

Confederate camp, probably on the north side of Pensacola Bay in the vicinity of Fort Barrancas.

Camp Roberts

A camp occupied by the 7th Vermont Regiment, located on the mainland near Fort Barrancas. Named for Colonel George T. Roberts of that regiment.

Camp Saufley

Temporary camp established by the NAS on Santa Rosa Island, opposite the station, in 1917-18. It was used as a seaplane base and gunnery range.

Camp Seward

A Union troop camp on Santa Rosa Island east of Fort Pickens. Battery Totten was located within the boundaries of this camp. Named in honor of William H. Seward, Secretary of State.

Camp Stoughton

A Union troop camp on Santa Rosa Island, near Fort Pickens. Occupied by the 7th Vermont Regiment. Named for Colonel Stoughton of the 4th Vermont Regiment.

Camp Union

In a letter book kept at Fort Pickens, 1861-64, a letter from the Post Adjutant, Fort Pickens, dated June 14, 1861, is addressed to a Captain of troops at Camp Union, and concerns the use of soldiers in work details. Presumably, this was an encampment of Federal troops on Santa Rosa Island in the vicinity of Fort Pickens.

Camp Walton

A Confederate troop camp located near the Indian Mound in Fort Walton Beach, Florida.

Camp Ward

This was an association of Confederate Veterans of Pensacola, Florida.

Canal Field (in Alabama)

NAS auxiliary field located between Wolf's Bay and Bon Secours Bay. No longer in use.

Cantonment Clinch

Located at Galvez Spring at the head of Bayou Chico near the end of present Z Street. The Spanish forces under Galvez camped here in 1781. American troops under General Jackson camped here in 1821, and the site continued to be used by U.S. Army troops in the 1820-30s. Named for General Duncan L. Clinch. (See Camp Hope and Camp Brady.)

Cantonment, Florida

The town of Cantonment is on the site of encampments of General Jackson's troops in 1814, while on a punitive expedition against the Spanish and in 1821, while awaiting the transfer of Florida to him as provisional governor.

Casa Fuerte

This structure, which appears to be a blockhouse, is shown on maps of Pensacola in the second Spanish period, 1781-1821. It was located between Government and Main Streets in the area now occupied by the Escambia County Utilities Authority sewage plant.

Chevalier Field

An NAS airfield located at Tartar Point on the station. Named in honor of Lieutenant Commander Godfrey de C. Chevalier, Naval Aviator No. 7. No longer used as an airfield. (See Station Field.)

Choctaw Field

NAS auxiliary field located in Choctawhatchee National Forest northeast of East Bay.

City Field

Name applied to the former location of Corry Field which was near Davis Highway and Texar Drive. The term "Old Corry Field" was also used.

Civil War Stockade in Pensacola (Redoubt)

In the summer of 1862, the 7th Regiment Vermont Volunteers built a log and sand stockade in the form of a redoubt near St. Michael's Cemetery.

Commodore's Pond

Fresh water pond in the Navy Yard used to store live oak logs and timbers. Located where a part of Chevalier Field was built.

Corry Field

Located on the north side of Bayou Grande and west of Pensacola. The first Corry Field which was dedicated in 1922, was originally called Kiwanis Field and was located on East Texar Drive. It was moved to the new location in 1927. Named in honor of LCDR William M. Corry, Jr., Naval Aviator No. 23, and the first Floridian to enter the flight training program at Pensacola. He was awarded the Medal of Honor, posthumously. This field is no longer active.

Corry Field, Jr.

The portion of the Corry Field reservation on the south side of U.S. Highway 98 is named on some maps as Corry Field, Jr. No longer in use.

Crescent Redoubt

Part of the Fort George fortifications. Was called Queen's Redoubt by the British and Fort San Bernardo by the Spanish.

Ellyson Field

A Naval Auxiliary Air Station field located on the Escambia Bay north of Interstate 10. Commissioned on January 20, 1943, it was named in honor of CDR Theodore G. Ellyson, Naval Aviator No. 1. This field was converted to an industrial park.

Faircloth Field (in Alabama)

NAS auxiliary field located northwest of Lillian, Alabama. No longer in use.

Felton's Field

NAS auxiliary field located in the Bellview area. Renamed Saufley Field in 1939.

Florida Point, Camp at

See Camp at Florida Point.

Forrest Sherman Field

Airfield on the Naval Air Station. Named for Admiral Forrest P. Sherman, Chief of Naval Operations.

Fort Arruinado (Fuerta Aruinado)

Referred to in a typescript, "History of Old Spanish Forts," prepared under auspices of the Works Progress Administration, on file in UWF Library. Also located on Map #140-17, Pensacola Historical Society as Fuerto Aruinado (Ruined Fort) at the western tip of Santa Rosa Island. In the Clubbs Manuscripts on file in the Pensacola Historical Museum it is stated to be, "a brick fort, constructed by the Spanish between 1781-96, on Santa Rosa Island opposite the present location of NAS. It was a brick fort. Exact location is not known and the site is now under water." (See Fort

Montagorda.)
Note: The Spanish word meaning "to ruin," "to wreck" is ARRUINAR.

Fort Barrancas
One of the four forts built for the defense of Pensacola Bay and the Navy Yard. Built 1839-44. Located on the Barrancas and near to, if not on top of, the original Spanish and British forts at that site.

Fort George
Built by the British on Gage Hill, approximately 1,200 yards north of the settlement of Pensacola. Construction started in 1779. It was captured by the Spanish under Galvez in 1781.

Fort Hodgson
A small log and earth fortification built by the 7th Alabama Cavalry commanded by Colonel Joseph Hodgson at Gonzalez, Florida (Fifteen-mile House). In a battle fought on July 22, 1864, Union troops under the command of Brigadier General Alexander Sandor Asboth defeated the Confederate forces and destroyed the fort.

Fort McClellan
A Union fortification in the vicinity of Lee Square in Pensacola. Built by the 6th New York Infantry after the Confederates evacuated the town in 1862. When the Union troops were moved to Fort Barrancas, 1863, this fort was probably abandoned.

Fort McRee
One of the four forts built by the United States for the defense of Pensacola Bay and the Navy Yard. It was begun in 1834 and completed in 1837. Located on Foster's Bank on the west side of the entrance channel to the bay, it was named for Lieutenant Colonel William McRee, U.S. Army, Corps fo Engineers. It was severely damaged by the Union bombardments of November, 1861 and January, 1962, and was not repaired after the Civil War ended. The site of this fort is now under water.

Fort Montagorda
This fort is mentioned in Edwin C. Bearss' "Historical Report on Fort Pickens" typescript manuscript. Ruins, consisting of hard dark sandstone, were mentioned in a report by the United States Board after a visit to Pensacola in 1822. The location was given as "on north shore of Santa Rosa Island about two miles from its western tip." The authors have not found other references to this fort.

Fort of "Santa Barbara"
This is the name given to a fort the Spanish proposed to build on or near the site of Fort San Miguel in Pensacola. It is referred to in a "Map of the bay and fort of Sta. Maria de Galbe...," dated March 12, 1756, and a "Plan of the Garrison 'San Miguel de Panzacola'," dated September 2, 1763. No record has been found that indicates this fort was built.

Fort Pickens
One of the four forts built by the United States for the defense of Pensacola Bay and the Navy Yard. Construction started in 1829, and was completed in 1835. Located on the western end of Santa Rosa Island at Point Siguenza, it was named for Brigadier General Andrew Pickens of the South Carolina State Troops in the American Revolution. Fort Pickens is now part of the Gulf Islands National Seashore and is administered by the National Park Service.

Fort Principe de Austurias
See Austurias, Fort Principe de.

Fort Redoubt
See Advanced Redoubt of Fort Barrancas.

Fort San Bernardo
Spanish name for the Queen's Redoubt which was a part of the Fort George fortifications.

Fort San Carlos de Austria

Name given to the first fort built on Barranca of Saint Thomas. The probable location was on the dune ridge, between Barrancas and Slemmer Avenues, on the Naval Air Station. Construction was started by the Spanish in 1698. It was razed by the French in September, 1719.

Fort San Carlos de Barrancas

A Spanish fortification built of pine logs and sand in 1797-98, on the Barrancas overlooking the entrance to Pensacola Bay. This was on the site of earlier Spanish and British fortifications and the site of present day Fort Barrancas.

Fort St. Michael

This is the British name for Fort San Miguel.

Fort San Miguel

Located on the site of or near to Seville Square in Pensacola. First built as a small blockhouse, garrisoned by nine soldiers, in 1740-50, to protect mission Indians from their enemies. When the Spanish presidio on Santa Rosa Island (Santa Rosa Punta de Siguenza) was abandoned in 1756, San Miguel became the presidio. At this time it was named San Miguel de las Amarillas, but in 1757, an order by the King of Spain, changed the name of the presidio to Panzacola.

When the Spanish took Florida from the British in 1781, they renamed Fort George, Fort San Miguel.

Fort Santa Rosa

Name given in American dispatches of 1814, to the Spanish Battery at Point Siguenza on Santa Rosa Island.

Fort Sombrero

The Spanish name given to the Prince of Wales Redoubt after they had taken Fort George and its two redoubts from the British, in 1781.

Fort Waldeck

Another name applied to the hornwork of Fort George, probably because Waldeck soldiers were used in the construction and during the defense when attacked by the Spanish under Galvez in 1781.

Fountain Field (Site 8A)

NAS auxiliary field located northwest of "K" Field. Now designated Site 8A.

Fuerte, Casa

See Casa Fuerte.

German's Field

NAS auxiliary field on the northwest side of the Pensacola Municipal Airport and contiguous with the airport. It is no longer in existence.

Gonzalez Field

NAS auxiliary field located in Gonzalez on the east side of U.S. Highway 29. No longer in use.

Harold Field

NAS auxiliary field located east of Milton, Florida.

Helm Field

NAS auxiliary field located northwest of Saufley Field. No longer in use.

Holley Field

NAS auxiliary field located on Santa Rosa peninsula, south of Holley, Florida.

"K" Field

NAS auxiliary field located near Gonzalez, Florida. It was also called King's Field. No longer in use.

Kaiser Field (in Alabama)

NAS auxiliary field located between Elberta and Lillian, Alabama. No longer in use.

Kings Field ("K" Field)

NAS auxiliary field located on the west side of U.S. Highway 29, and south of Cantonment, Florida.

Kiwanis Field (Corry Field, City Field)

The name given to the approximately one mile square area near Goulding (on East Texar Boulevard between 9th Avenue and Davis Highway), which later became the first Corry Field. In 1920, the Pensacola Kiwanis Club had the land cleared and paid the rent for about two years anticipating that the Navy Department would require it for expansion of training facilities for land planes.

Lyons Field

NAS auxiliary field located north of Cottage Hill, Florida, and on the west side of U.S. Highway 29. No longer in use.

Magnolia Field (in Alabama)

NAS auxiliary field located northwest of Foley, Alabama. No longer in use.

Middle Redoubt

Another name given to the Prince of Wales Redoubt; part of the Fort George fortifications.

Middleton Field (in Alabama)

NAS auxiliary field located near Evergreen, Alabama.

Milton Field

NAS auxiliary field located near Milton, Florida. No longer used by the Navy.

Municipal Field (Hagler Field)

In the 1930s the area where the present Pensacola Regional Airport is located was used by the Navy for land plane training. The Navy had constructed for its use, an administration building containing offices, storerooms, and student and instructor ready rooms. A fuel service system and a watch tower had also been installed.

Navy Reservation (Reserve)

Land belonging to the United States Navy, lying between Pensacola Bay and Bayou Grande which includes the site of the Navy Yard and the present site of Forrest Sherman Field.

Navy Yard at Pensacola

Located at Tartar Point in Pensacola Bay. Founded in 1825, it was closed in 1911. The villages of Woolsey and Warrington adjoined on the north and west respectively. Woolsey was partly destroyed during the Civil War, was rebuilt and occupied until taken over by the Navy in the 1920s. Warrington, also badly damaged in the Civil War, was rebuilt and continued to exist until relocated by the Navy in the 1930s. The Navy Yard was placed on caretaker status in 1911, and was reopened by the Navy as a training base and air station in 1914.

Noble's Stockade (Noble's Fort)

James Noble arrived in Pensacola in 1763, and became the local representative of a trading company of prominent Englishmen. He built a stockade which consisted of a single palisade enclosing a two story house and several other buildings, located in the block south of present day Government Street and west of the Escambia County Judicial Building. This stockade is pictured in a drawing, "A View of Pensacola in West Florida," published during the British period, 1763-81.

Oakfield

A small community 6 miles north of Pensacola. The Confederate forces maintained picket lines in the area in 1863-64 and there was some skirmishing between them and the Federal troops.

Old Corry Field
See City Field.

Old Spanish Fort Battery
Located east of Battery Lincoln on north side of Santa Rosa Island. This battery was installed after the Battle of Santa Rosa Island. Armament: one 10-inch Parrot Gun (rifled).

Pace Field
NAS auxiliary field located north of Pace, Florida.

Perdido Field (in Alabama)
NAS auxiliary field located southwest of Lillian, Alabama. No longer in use.

Pine Barren Creek
A Confederate picket camp, one of several outposts guarding a Confederate depot at Pollard, Alabama. Attacked and dispersed by troops of the 2nd Maine Regiment in December, 1864.

Pine Hill
A Spanish artillery position used in the siege of Fort George in 1781.

Point Siguenza on Santa Rosa Island
The western tip of Santa Rosa Island, named by the Spanish Point Siguenza, was a logical place for a fortification to defend the entrance to Pensacola Bay. It was first fortified by the Spanish in 1719, but this little stockaded battery was destroyed by the French that same year. It was occupied intermittently by the British between 1763 and 1781. Reconstructed by the Spanish about 1793, this battery was destroyed by the British in 1814. The next fortification to be built here was Fort Pickens (1829), followed in turn by the Endicott System gun emplacements (1890-1910), and the gun batteries and other defense installations of World Wars I and II.

Post of Fort Barrancas
Name given to the camp for troops manning Forts Pickens, McRee, Barrancas, and Redoubt. Later, formally established as a Coast Artillery Post, Headquarters of the 13th Coast Artillery, and also the command center for the Coast Artillery defense of Pensacola Bay.

Prince of Wales Redoubt
Part of the fortifications of Fort George on Gage Hill. It was also called the Middle Redoubt. The Spanish renamed it Fort Sombrero, after they took Fort George in 1781.

Queen's Redoubt
The outer redoubt of the Fort George fortifications. It was also called the Crescent Redoubt. The Spanish renamed it Fort Bernardo after they took Fort George in 1781.

Redoubt
This was a wood and sand redoubt built by the 7th Vermont Volunteers in 1862. It was located near St. Michael's Cemetery in Pensacola. (See Civil War Stockade in Pensacola.)

Redoubt
See Advanced Redoubt of Fort Barrancas.

Redoubt (East of Pensacola)
An undated map of Pensacola in the British period (1763-1781), shows a redoubt on the east side of the town near the bay shore. This redoubt, which was located in the general area where Eighth Avenue and Zaragosa Street intersect, is reported to have been constructed by the citizens of the town.

Royal Navy Redoubt (Red Cliffs, Upper and Lower Batteries)
A British fortification located on the present site of Fort Barrancas. Construction started in 1771. After the Spanish took control of Florida from the British in 1783, they renamed it Fort San Carlos de Barrancas.

San Carlos

A name used incorrectly for the Battery San Antonio. The confusion arises from the fact that the old Fort San Carlos de Barrancas was located beneath the present Fort Barrancas.

Santa Rosa Field

NAS auxiliary field located east of Milton, Florida.

Santa Rosa Punta de Siguenza

The second Spanish fort (stockade) on Santa Rosa Island. It was located approximately three-fourths of a mile east of Point Siguenza, on the north side of the island. Destroyed by a storm in 1752.

Saufley Field

Naval Auxiliary Air Station located west of Pensacola, between Lillian and Mobile Highways. Built 1939-40. Named in honor of Lieutenant (Junior Grade) Richard C. Saufley, Naval Aviator No. 14, killed in a crash while on an endurance record flight. (See Felton's Field.)

Scholl's Pond

Fresh water pond on the Navy Yard in which live oak logs and timbers were stored. Located north of the Chevalier Field, it is now filled in.

Silverhill Field (in Alabama)

NAS auxiliary field located west of Robertsdale, Alabama.

Spanish Battery

A term sometimes used in referring to Battery San Antonio.

Spanish Stodado (Stocado)

An early Spanish fort or stockade located on the Escambia River about 28 miles from Pensacola. Little seems to be known about its location, when it was built or how long it was used.

Spanish Redoubts on Bayou Chico

Two timber redoubts built by Galvez in 1781 one on each side of Bayou Chico, during the siege of the British at Fort George.

Spencer Field

NAS auxiliary field located northwest of Pace, Florida.

Station Field

Located on the Naval Air Station, 1915-1921. Was originally the field used by lighter-than-air craft. Was enlarged in 1921-22, for use by land planes, and renamed Chevalier Field.

Stump Field

NAS auxiliary field located north of Bell's Field. No longer in use.

Summerdale Field (in Alabama)

NAS auxiliary field located north of Foley, Alabama.

Tartar Point (Punta de Aguero)

Site of a British blockhouse built in 1771, and destroyed by them just before Galvez landed his troops to begin the siege of Fort George in 1781. The Naval Air Station now covers Tartar Point.

Tar Kiln Field

NAS auxiliary field located west of Bronson Field near Perdido Bay. It was later incorporated into Bronson Field.

Unfinished Redoubts

A map by Joseph Purcell, "A Plan of Pensacola and its Environs in the Present State," dated 1778, shows three "unfinished redoubts" in Pensacola. One was on the west side of the Fort at Pensacola (stockade in the center of the town), approximately where Baylen and Government

Streets intersect. The other two were north of the Fort, near the intersections of Intendencia and Palafox Streets, and Intendencia and Alcaniz Streets. It is not known if these structures were completed and armed.

U.S.S. *Lexington*, CVT-16

Aircraft carrier assigned to the Naval Air Station for training aviators. Commissioned February 17, 1943. Assigned to NAS, Pensacola, December 29, 1963.

Upper and Lower Batteries

See Royal Navy Redoubt.

"V" Field

NAS auxiliary field located west of Pensacola, north of Lillian Highway. No longer in use.

Water Battery

See Battery San Antonio.

Water Battery at Fort Barrancas

Another name for Battery San Antonio; so called because it is at water level. This name is often used today.

Water Battery of Fort McRee

A battery located on Foster's Bank to the south of Fort McRee.

Water Battery of Fort Pickens

In May, 1864, rumors came to the Union forces at Fort Pickens that the Confederates were planning an attack by the ironclad ship *Tennessee* then in Mobile Bay. This resulted in the construction of a "water battery" on the end of Santa Rosa Island. 11-inch and 15-inch guns were mounted to command the channel entrance into Pensacola Bay.

Whiting Field

Naval Auxiliary Air Station, located north of Milton, Florida. Built 1942-43. Named in honor of Captain Kenneth Whiting, Naval Aviator No. 16, first to command naval aviation units overseas in World War I, first acting commander of the Navy's first carrier, and leader in the development of carriers.

Wolf Field

NAS auxiliary field located between Wolf's Bay and Perdido Bay.

"X" Field

NAS auxiliary field located near Mobile Highway, between Eight-Mile and Seven-Mile Creeks. No longer in use.

"Y" Field

NAS auxiliary field located west of Pensacola, north of Lillian Highway. No longer in use.

"Z" Field

NAS auxiliary field located west of Pensacola, north of Lillian Highway. No longer in use.

Sources for List of Posts, Camps, Stations, Fields, Batteries, and Other Military Installations

Alison, Joseph Dill. "Civil War Diary." Pensacola Historical Society Quarterly, 2 (January, 1966).

Appleyard, John. Pensacola: The French-Spanish Confrontation, 1660-1720. Pensacola: Pensacola Home and Savings Association, 1976.

Babcock, Willoughby, Jr. Selections from the Letters and Diaries of Brevet Brigadier General Willoughby Babcock. Bulletin 2, issued by Division of Archives and History, War of the Rebellion Series, Albany: University of the State of New York, 1922.

Baker, Henry A. "Archaeological Investigations at Fort George, Pensacola, Fla." Miscellaneous Project Report, Series No. 34. Tallahassee: Division of Archives, Florida Department of State, 1975.

Bearss, Edwin C. "Civil War Operations In and Around Pensacola." Florida Historical Quarterly 36, No. 2 (October, 1957), pp. 125-165.

— "Historic Structure Report...Fort Barrancas, 1977." Manuscript on file at the Gulf Islands National Seashore Library.

— "Historic Structure Report...Fort Pickens..." 1976. Manuscript on file at the Gulf Islands National Seashore Library.

— "Historic Structure Report...Fort Pickens and Endicott Battery" 1979. Manuscript on file at the Gulf Islands National Seashore Library.

Brown, Dot. "Cantonment Clinch," Pensacola Journal, April 7, 1974.

"Camp Ward Constitution and By-Laws, Confederate Veterans, Pensacola, Florida." On file at the Pensacola Historical Museum.

Caughey, John W. Bernardo de Galvez in Louisiana, 1776-1783. Berkeley: University of California Press, 1934.

Civil War Round Table of Pensacola. Florida in the Civil War — 1860 Through Reconstruction. Pensacola: 1961.

Civil War Times Illustrated, Vol. 7, No. 4, July, 1968.

Clubb, Occie, "Papers." Manuscript collection, Pensacola Historical Museum.

Coker, William S. and Coker, Hazel P. The Siege of Pensacola, 1781, in Maps. Pensacola: Perdido Bay Press, 1981.

Davis, D. Douglass; Parks, Virginia; and Vickers, Elizabeth D. "Fort Barrancas, 1875," Pensacola Historical Society Quarterly, Summer, 1974, pp. 1-35.

Deutsch, Dianne Karlstein. "Andrew Jackson's Invasion of Spanish Florida." PhD dissertation, University of Maine, 1971.

Escarosa Humanities Center. Federal Project. Documents filed at the Pensacola Historical Museum.

Faye, Stanley. "The Spanish and British Fortifications of Pensacola, 1781-1821," Florida Historical Quarterly 20, No. 2 and 3 (October, 1941; January, 1942), pp. 151-168; 277-292.

Federal Writers' Project. "History of Old Spanish Forts." Typescript on file at the University of West Florida Library.

Gosport, Feb. 18, 1944; June 17, 1959.

Hoag, David D. Life and Letters of Capt. David D. Hoag, comp. by J.C. Hoag. New York, 1866.

Hollbrook, William C. "A Narrative of the Services of the Officers and Enlisted Men of the 7th Regiment of Vermont Volunteers," 1882. Manuscript collection, Pensacola Historical Museum.

Ingersoll — Iowa and the Rebellion, J.P. Lippincott & Co., 1866.

Letters — Department of Florida and Successor Commands — April, 1861 - January, 1869. Microfilm, Gulf Islands National Seashore Library.

Lovelace, S.L. Letter to the authors, "U.S. Navy Outlying Landing Fields," March 8, 1982.

Conrad A. Lusk, Letter to his sister from Camp Chalmers, Warrington, Florida, December 9, 1961. Pensacola Historical Museum, Manuscript Collection.

McGovern, James, ed. Andrew Jackson and Pensacola. Pensacola: Bicentennial Series, 1974.

North Atlantic Squadron in Camp, April, 1888, Brig. Gen. O.F. Heyerman, Commanding. New York, E.H. Hart Naval and Military Photographer and Publisher, n.d.

Parks, Virginia; Rich, Alan; and Simons, Norman. "Pensacola in the Civil War," Pensacola Historical Society Quarterly 9, No. 2 (Spring, 1978), 3-44.

Pearce, George F. The U.S. Navy in Pensacola; From Sailing Ships to Naval Aviation, 1825-1930. Gainesville: University Presses of Florida, 1980.

Pensacola's Historical Markers. Pensacola: Municipal Advertising Board, n.d.

"Pictorial History of the Naval Air Station at Pensacola" Scrapbook prepared by L.W. Parrish. Naval Air Station Library.

Romans, Bernard. A Concise Natural History of East and West Florida, Facsimile reproduction of the 1775 Edition - Gainesville, 1962, University of Florida Press.

Rush, N. Orwin, Spain's Final Triumph over Great Britain in the Gulf of Mexico: The Battle of Pensacola, March 9 to May 8, 1781 (Tallahassee: Florida State University, 1966).

Rumph, Langdon L., "Letters of a Teenage Confederate," Florida Historical Quarterly 38, No. 4 (April, 1960), pp. 340-346.

Santa Rosa News Boy. Vol. 1, No. 2, June 15, 1863.

Skinner, Woodward B., Geronimo at Fort Pickens (Pensacola: Frank R. Parkhurst & Son, 1981).

Simons, Norman. "The Pensacola Fortifications," Siege! Spain and Britain: Battle of Pensacola, ed. Virginia Parks. Pensacola: Pensacola Historical Society, 1981, pp. 45-54.

Slemmer, Adam J. "Letterbook kept at Fort Pickens, 1861-1864, with correspondence of Lt. Slemmer and Captain H.A. Allen, in charge of Union forces." Photocopy, University of West Florida Library.

Starr, J. Barton, Tories, Dons, and Rebels (Gainesville: University Presses of Florida, 1976).

Sutton, Mrs. Leora M., Personal notes pertaining to historic structures in Pensacola.

United States Naval Aviation, 1900-1970. NAVAIR 00-80P-1. Washington: Government Printing Office, 1970.

Whitman, William E.S. and True, Charles H. Maine in the War for the Union. Lewiston, Maine: Nelson Dingley, Jr. and Company, 1865.

Maps and Drawings

Drawings of Fort McRee. Pensacola Historical Museum.

Map. "Fort Pickens, Florida." June 10, 1861. Gulf Islands National Seashore Library.

Map. "Naval Air Training Bases, Pensacola, Florida. Naval Air Station, Naval Auxiliary Stations, and Outlying Practice Fields." [1940s.]

Map. "Outlying Landing Fields, Naval Air Station, Pensacola, Florida." June 30, 1938. Pensacola Historical Museum.

Map. "Outlying Landing Fields, Naval Air Training Bases." June 30, 1947. Pensacola Historical Museum.

Map. "Pensacola, A City of Heritage in Its 5th Century." Pensacola-Escambia Development Commission and the Galvez Commission. [1981.]

Pintado, Vicente, "Florida Occidental, Partido de Panzacola, Ano de 1817" Pensacola Historical Museum Map File.

Purcell, Joseph, "A Plan of Pensacola and its Environs in its Present State," dated 1770. Pensacola Historical Museum Map File.

Undated map of Pensacola in the British Period (1763-1781), Pensacola Historical Museum Map File.

Glossary of Military Terms

Barbette: Within a fortification, a mound of earth or platform on which guns are mounted, allowing firing over the parapet instead of through embrasures.

Bastion: A projecting portion of a rampart or fortification that stands out from the corners.

Battery: A grouping of artillery pieces for tactical purposes.

Blockhouse: A structure of heavy timbers formerly used for military defense with sides loopholed and pierced for gunfire, often with projecting upper story.

Cantonment: A temporary encampment for troops.

Casemate: A vault or chamber, especially in a rampart, with embrasures for cannons and other artillery.

Cordon: A projecting band of stone on the surface of a wall.

Counterscarp: The exterior slope or wall of the ditch.

Covered Way: A position or situation affording protection from enemy fire. Usually a level area near a fortification used for troops to patrol or assemble.

Curtain: The part of a wall or rampart connecting two neighboring bastions.

Demi-Bastion: Half a bastion or fort.

Ditch: An excavated area in front of, or near the parapet. Serves as an obstacle to the assailant.

Embrasure: An opening in a wall through which artillery may be discharged, with the sides of the opening usually flaring outward.

Emplacement: A prepared position for weapons or military equipment. Putting into position.

Enceinte: The line of works enclosing a fortified place; the space so enclosed.

Fascines: A long bundle of sticks bound together and used for such purposes as filling ditches or making parapets.

Glacis: A gentle slope; an incline that runs downward from a fortification.

Hornwork: An addition to a corner of a fort, composed of two demi-bastions joined by a curtain.

Magazine: A well-protected room in which powder or other explosives are kept in a fort.

Palisade: A fence of stakes for defense. A long, strong stake pointed at the top, set close to others as a defense.

Parade: The level space forming the interior or enclosed area of a fortification.

Parapet: A wall, rampart, or elevation of earth or stone to protect soldiers; also a breastwork, a low wall to protect the edge of a platform.

Pintle: A pin or bolt on which some other part pivots or turns.

Presidio: A garrison or fortified place. Usually includes buildings beyond the stockade.

Rampart: A broad embankment, raised as a fortification, usually surmounted by parapets.

Redan: A fortification composed of two low walls joined at an angle pointed outward.

Redoubt: A small, enclosed fort used in fortifying tops of hills or approaches to larger fortifications.

Sally Port: A gateway permitting the passage of a large number of troops at one time.

Scarp: The inner side or wall of a ditch surrounding a rampart.

Spike: To make a cannon unusable by driving a metal spike into the hole where the powder is ignited.

Stockade: A line of stout posts set firmly to form a defense. An enclosure or pen made with posts and stakes.

Terraplain, Terreplein: The top, platform, or horizontal surface of a rampart, on which the cannon are placed.

References

[1] Carlos de Siguenza, "Siguenza's Report," Colonial Penscola, ed. James McGovern (Pensacola, 1974), p. 51.

[2] Stanley Faye, "The Spanish and British Fortifications of Pensacola, 1698-1821," Florida Historical Quarterly 20, No. 2 and 3 (October, 1941; January, 1942), pp. 151-152.

[3] Albert Manucy, "The Founding of Pensacola — Reason and Reality," Florida Historical Quarterly, 37, No. 3-4 (January and April, 1959), p. 230.

[4] Stanley Faye, "The Contest for Pensacola Bay and Other Gulf Ports, 1698-1722," Florida Historical Quarterly, 24, No. 3-4 (January and April, 1946), p. 174.

[5] Manucy, "The Founding of Pensacola," pp. 229-236.

[6] William Edward Dunn, Spanish and French Rivalry in the Gulf Region of the United States, 1698-1702. (Freeport, N.Y.: Books for Libraries Press, 1971), p. 179.

[7] Faye, "The Spanish and British Fortifications," pp. 153-154.

[8] Manucy, "The Founding of Pensacola," p. 232.

[9] Faye, "The Spanish and British Fortifications," pp. 152-155.

[10] Manucy, "The Founding of Pensacola," p. 240.

[11] Faye, "The Spanish and British Fortifications," p. 153.

[12] Manucy, "The Founding of Pensacola," pp. 240-241.

[13] Ibid., p. 239.

[14] Faye, "The Spanish and British Fortifications," p. 153.

[15] Ibid., p. 155.

[16] William B. Griffin, "Spanish Pensacola, 1700-1763," Florida Historical Quarterly 37, No. 3-4 (January and April, 1959), pp. 247-248.

[17] Ibid., p. 246.

[18] Faye, "The Spanish and British Fortifications," pp. 154-155.

[19] Manucy, "The Founding of Pensacola," p. 238.

[20] Faye, "The Spanish and British Fortifications," p. 156.

[21] Griffin, "Spanish Pensacola," p. 252.

[22] Faye, "The Spanish and British Fortifications," pp. 156-158.

[23] John Appleyard, Pensacola: The French-Spanish Confrontation, 1660-1720. (Pensacola: Pensacola Home and Savings Association, 1976). Unpaged.

[24] Faye, "The Contest for Pensacola Bay," p. 190.

[25] Faye, "The Spanish and British Fortifications," p. 158.

[26] Faye, "The Contest for Pensacola Bay," pp. 307-313.

[27] Appleyard, "Pensacola: The French-Spanish Confrontation."

[28] Griffin, "Spanish Pensacola," p. 255.

[29] Faye, "The Spanish and British Fortifications," pp. 158-160.

[30] Griffin, "Spanish Pensacola," pp. 255-256.

[31] Ernest P. Dibble, ed. Spain and Her Rivals on the Gulf Coast. (Pensacola: Historic Pensacola Preservation Board, 1971), pp. 70-71.

[32] Faye, "The Spanish and British Fortifications," pp. 162-163.

[33] Pedro de Rivera, Report on the Presidio of Punta de Siguenza, Alias Panzacola, 1744. ed. William S. Coker. (Pensacola: Pensacola Historical Society, 1975), pp. 6-14.

[34] Dibble, Spain and Her Rivals, p. 70.

[35] William S. Coker, "The Financial History of Pensacola's Spanish Presidios, 1698-1763," Pensacola Historical Quarterly 9, (Spring, 1979), p. 5.

[36] Faye, "The Spanish and British Fortifications," p. 162.

[37] Griffin, "Spanish Pensacola," pp. 260-262.

[38] Faye, "The Spanish and British Fortifications," p. 162.

[39] Ibid., p. 167.

[40] Griffin, "Spanish Pensacola," pp. 260-262.

[41] Coker, "The Financial History of Pensacola's Spanish Presidios," p. 8.

[42] Cecil Johnson, "Pensacola in the British Period: Summary and Significance," Florida Historical Quarterly 37, No. 3-4 (January and April, 1959), pp. 263-266.

[43] Robert R. Rea, "Pensacola Under the British (1763-1781)," Colonial Pensacola, ed. James McGovern (Pensacola, 1974), p. 59.

[44] Norman Simons, "The Pensacola Fortifications," Siege! Spain and Britain: Battle of Pensacola, ed. Virginia Parks (Pensacola: Pensacola Historical Society, 1981), p. 45.

[45] Rea, "Pensacola Under the British," p. 60.

[46] Faye, "The Spanish and British Fortifications," p. 278.

[47] Robert R. Rea, "Brigadier Frederick Haldimand," Florida Historical Quarterly 54, No. 4 (April, 1976), pp. 522-523.

[48] Map, "Plan & Section of the Upper & Lower Batteries, Laid Out and Begun Building, 5th March, 1771, for protecting the Harbor of Pensacola." On file at the Pensacola Historical Museum.

[49] Clinton Newton Howard, "Colonial Pensacola: The British Period," Florida Historical Quarterly 19, No. 4 (April, 1941), pp. 374-387.

[50] J. Barton Starr, Tories, Dons, and Rebels (Gainesville: University Presses of Florida, 1976), p. 57.

[51] Johnson, "Pensacola in the British Period," p. 277.

[52] Starr, Tories, Dons, and Rebels, p. 184.

[53] Simons, "The Pensacola Fortifications," p. 46.

[54] Cecil Johnson, British West Florida, 1763-1781 (New Haven: Yále University Press, 1943), p. 155.

[55] Simons, "The Pensacola Fortifications," pp. 45-46.

[56] Starr, Tories, Dons and Rebels," p. 184.

[57] Simons, "The Pensacola Fortifications," p. 47.

[58] Frederick Cubberly, "Fort George (St. Michael) Pensacola," Florida Historical Quarterly 6, No. 4 (April, 1928), p. 220.

[59] Simons, "The Pensacola Fortifications," pp. 47-50.

[60] Faye, "The Spanish and British Fortifications," p. 279.

[61] Simons, "The Pensacola Fortifications," pp. 46-47.

[62] N. Orwin Rush, Spain's Triumph over Great Britain in the Gulf of Mexico: The Battle of Pensacola, March 9 to May 8, 1781 (Tallahassee: Florida State University, 1966), p. 4, n.

[63] Starr, Tories, Dons and Rebels, pp. 186-187.

[64] Faye, "The Spanish and British Fortifications," p. 278.

[65] Starr, Tories, Dons, and Rebels, pp. 186-187.

[66] Max von Eelking, The German Allies in the American Revolution, 1776-1783 (Baltimore: Genealogical Publishing Company, 1969), p. 223.

[67] Robert R. Rea and James A. Servies, The Log of the H.M.S. Mentor (Gainesville: University Presses of Florida, 1982), pp. 1-31.

[68] Eelking, The German Allies, pp. 218-223.

[69] Starr, Tories, Dons, and Rebels," p. 187.

[70] Faye, "The Spanish and British Fortifications," p. 279.

[71] Virginia Parks, "The Siege of Pensacola" Seige! Spain and Britain: Battle of Pensacola, ed. Virginia Parks (Pensacola: Pensacola Historical Society, 1981), p. 61.

[72] Faye, "The Spanish and British Fortifications," p. 278.

[73] Eelking, The German Allies, p. 31.

[74] Rush, Spain's Final Triumph, p. 83.

[75] Parks, "The Siege of Pensacola," p. 60.

[76] Simons, "The Pensacola Fortifications," p. 46.

[77] Parks, "The Siege of Pensacola," p. 64.

[78] Simons, "The Pensacola Fortifications," p. 52.

[79] Rush, Spain's Final Triumph, p. 14.

[80] William S. Coker and G. Douglass Inglais, The Spanish Censuses of Pensacola, 1784-1820: A Geneological Guide to Spanish Pensacola (Pensacola: Perdido Bay Press, 1980), p. 145.

[81] Jack D.J. Holmes, "Pensacola: Spanish Dominion, 1781-1821," Colonial Pensacola, ed. James McGovern (Pensacola, 1974), p. 93.

[82] Starr, Tories, Dons, and Rebels, p. 199, n.

[83] Faye, "The Spanish and British Fortifications," pp. 284-286.

[84] Willard B. Robinson, American Forts (Urbana: University of Illinois Press, 1977), p. 61.

[85] HABS No. Fla.-144. "Bateria de San Antonio," p. 3.

[86] Handwritten memo on file at the Gulf Islands National Seashore Library. No author given.

[87] HABS No. Fla.-144. "Bateria de San Antonio," p. 3.

[87] HABS No. Fla.-144. "Bateria de San Antonio," p. 3.

[88] Faye, "The Spanish and British Fortifications," p. 285.

[89] Edwin C. Bearss, "Historic Structure Report...Fort Barrancas, 1977." Manuscript on file at Gulf Islands National Seashore Library, p. 5.

[90] Faye, "The Spanish and British Fortifications," p. 285.

[91] Shows on no plans of the fort.

[92] David H. White, "A View of Spanish West Florida: Selected Letters of Governor Juan Vicente Folch," Florida Historical Quarterly 56, No. 2 (October, 1977), p. 140.

[93] Bearss, "Historic Structures Report...Barrancas," p. 55.

[94] John Pope, A Tour Through the Southern and Western Territories, Richmond, 1792; reprinted, New York, 1888). Quoted by Jack D.L. Holmes in "Pensacola: Spanish Dominion, 1781-1821," Colonial Pensacola, ed. James McGovern (Pensacola, 1974), p. 95.

[95] L.N. McAlister, "Pensacola During the Second Spanish Period," Florida Historical Quarterly 37, No. 3-4 (January and April, 1959), pp. 312-317.

[96] John Innerarity, "Letters of John Innerarity," Florida Historical Quarterly 9, No. 3 (January, 1931), p. 128.

[97] John Innerarity, "Letters of John Innerarity," Florida Historical Quarterly 11, No. 3 (January, 1933), pp. 140-141.

[98] Faye, "The Spanish and British Fortifications," pp. 290-292.

[99] McAlister, "Pensacola During the Second Spanish Period," pp. 320-322.

[100] "The Defenses of Florida: A Report of Captain James Gadsden, Aide-de-Camp to General Andrew Jackson," Nashville, August 1, 1818. Original report from files of the Intelligence Division, Engineer Corps, War Department, Washington. Reprinted in Florida Historical Quarterly 15, No. 4 (April, 1937), pp. 242-243.

[101] "The Public Buildings of Pensacola, 1818." Document found in the Papers of Andrew Jackson, Division of Manuscripts, Library of Congress. Reprinted in Florida Historical Quarterly 16, No. 1 (July, 1937), pp. 45-47.

[102] Herbert J. Doherty, Jr., "Ante-Bellum Pensacola: 1821-1860," Florida Historical Quarterly 37, No. 3-4 (January and April, 1959), p. 337.

[103] T.T. Wentworth, Jr., "Pensacola Memorabilia," Florida Historical Quarterly 39, No. 1 (July, 1960), p. 149.

[104] Dot Brown, "Cantonment Clinch," Pensacola Journal, April 7, 1944, p. 1 E.

[105] Edwin C. Bearss, "Historic Structure Report... Fort Pickens." Manuscript on file at Gulf Islands National Seashore Library, p. 22.

[106] Emanuel Raymond Lewis, Seacoast Fortification of the United States: An Introductory History. (Washington: Smithsonian Institution Press, 1970), p. 37.

[107] George F. Pearce, The U.S. Navy in Pensacola: From Sailing Ships to Naval Aviation (1825-1930), (Gainesville: University Presses of Florida, 1980), pp. 16-17.

[108] "Fort Pickens — A Century of Change," a pamphlet published by the Gulf Islands National Seashore, n.d. Unpaged.

[109] Frederick C. Gjessing and John C. Garner, Jr., "Historic Structure Report — Architectural Section. Advanced Redoubt of Fort Barrancas." Unpublished report on file at the Gulf Islands National Seashore Library, 1975, p. 5.

[110] Pearce, The U.S. Navy in Pensacola, p. 17.

[111] Ernest F. Dibble, William H. Chase: Gulf Coast Fort Builder (Wilmington: Gulf Coast Collection, n.d.), unpaged.

[112] Bearss, "Historic Structure Report...Fort Pickens," pp. 92-121.

[113] Ernest F. Dibble, Antebellum Pensacola and the Military Presence. (Pensacola: Bicentennial Series, 1974), pp. 61-62.

[114] Bearss, "Historic Structure Report...Fort Pickens," p. 144.

[115] Ibid., p. 155.

[116] Ibid., pp. 161-163.

[117] Map, "Preliminary Chart to Entrance to Pensacola Bay," 1859. Copy in Gulf Islands National Seashore Library. Map, "Sketch of Foster's Bank and the Sites of Fort McRee and Advanced Battery," November 5, 1852. Copy in the Pensacola Historical Museum. Map, "Map of Fort McRee Showing South Battery," September 6, 1960. Copy in the Pensacola Historical Museum.

[118] Bearss, "Historic Structure Report...Fort Pickens," pp. 284-288.

[119] Ibid., pp. 289-290.

[120] Ibid., pp. 314-315.

[121] Ibid., pp. 311-312.

[122] Ibid., pp. 402-405.

[123] Ibid., pp. 410-411.

[124] Ibid., pp. 442-444.

[125] Map, "Gun Batteries, Pensacola Bay, 1861-62." Copy on file at the Gulf Islands National Seashore Library.

[126] Virginia Parks, Alan Rick, and Norman Simons, "Pensacola in the Civil War," Pensacola Historical Society Quarterly 9, No. 2 (Spring, 1978), pp. 17-18.

[127] Bearss, "Historic Structure Report...Fort Pickens," pp. 484-490.

[128] Parks, "Pensacola in the Civil War," p. 19.

[129] Bearss, "Historic Structure Report...Fort Pickens," p. 532.

[130] Bearss, "Historic Structure Report...Fort Barrancas," pp. 530-539.

[131] Bearss, "Historic Structure Report...Fort Pickens," p. 644.

[132] Lewis, "Seacoast Fortifications," p. 77.

[133] Bearss, "Historic Structure Report...Fort Barrancas," pp. 575-585.

[134] Edwin C. Bearss, "Historic Structure Report, Fort Pickens and the Endicott Battery," 2 vols. Unpublished report on file at Gulf Islands National Seashore Library. Vol. 1, p. 12.

[135] Robert B. Bradley, "Role of the Army in Pensacola, 1933-1941." Research paper on file at the University of West Florida Library. 1975. Unpaged.

[136] Bearss, "Historic Structure Report...Endicott Battery," Vol. 1, p. 166; Vol. 2, p. 197.

[137] Bradley, "Role of the Army in Pensacola," Unpaged.

[138] Bearss, "Historic Structure Report...Fort Barrancas," pp. 603-612.

[139] Ibid., p. 610.

[140] Ibid., p. 612.

[141] "Fort Pickens: A Century of Change," Unpaged.

[142] Dot Brown, Pensacola Journal, April 7, 1974, p. 1 E.

[143] Karl Bernhard, Travel Through North America

During the Years 1825 and 1826. (Philadelphia: Cary, Lea, and Cary, 1828), pp. 44-49.

[144] Map, "Santa Rosa Island, Indicating Location of Fort Pickens, Wharf, and Assistant Engineer's Quarters." Copy on file at the Pensacola Historical Museum.

[145] "Fort Pickens: A Century of Change." Unpaged.

[146] William H. Chase, "Memoir on the Defense of the Entrance of Pensacola Bay with the Description and Estimate of the Two Forts Recommended to Defend the Mainland," 1830. Typescript on file at the Gulf Islands National Seashore Library, pp. 2-8.

[147] "Fort Pickens: A Century of Change." Unpaged.

[148] Chase, "Memoir on the Defense of...Pensacola Bay," pp. 10-16.

[149] "Fort Pickens: A Century of Change." Unpaged.

[150] Bearss, "Historic Structure Report...Fort Pickens," pp. 205-207.

[151] "Fort Pickens: A Century of Change." Unpaged.

[152] Bearss, "Historic Structure Report...Fort Pickens," pp. 315-316.

[153] Ibid., p. 425.

[154] Ibid., p. 425.

[155] Ibid., p. 483, p. 493.

[156] Ibid., p. 447.

[157] Parks, "Pensacola in the Civil War," p. 18.

[158] Bearss, "Historic Structure Report...Fort Pickens," pp. 485-487.

[159] Ibid., p. 490.

[160] Ibid., p. 510.

[161] Ibid., p. 511-512.

[162] Ibid., p. 543.

[163] Ibid., pp. 550-551.

[164] Bearss, "Historic Structure Report...Fort Barrancas," pp. 507-510.

[165] Woodward B. Skinner, Geronimo at Fort Pickens. (Pensacola: Frank R. Parkhurst & Son, 1981), p. 5-16.

[166] Bearss, "Historic Structure Report...Endicott Battery," Vol. 2, pp. 218-230.

[167] Ibid., Vol. 2, p. 133.

[168] Ibid., Vol. 2, pp. 232-240.

[169] "Fort Pickens: A Century of Change," Unpaged.

[170] Pearce, The U.S. Navy in Pensacola, p. 40.

[171] Drawings, "Fortifications — Fort McRee." On file at the Pensacola Historical Museum.

[172] Chase, "Memoir on the Defense of...Pensacola Bay," p. 19.

[173] Drawings, "Fortifications — Fort McRee."

[174] Conrad A. Lusk, Letter to his sister from Camp Chalmers, Warrington, Florida, December 9, 1961. Pensacola Historical Museum, Manuscript Collection.

[175] Drawings, "Fortifications — Fort McRee."

[176] Bearss, "Historic Structure Report...Fort Pickens," p. 486.

[177] Staff, Gulf Islands National Seashore.

[178] Pearce, The U.S. Navy in Pensacola, p. 40.

[179] Drawings, "Fortifications — Fort McRee."

[180] Bearss, "Historic Structure Report...Fort Pickens," p. 486.

[181] Edwin C. Bearss, "Civil War Operations In and Around Pensacola," Florida Historical Quarterly 36, No. 2 (October, 1957), pp. 125-165; 39, No. 3 (January, 1961), pp. 231-255; 39, No. 4 (April, 1961), pp. 330-353, p. 123.

[182] Ibid., pp. 158-159.

[183] Ibid., pp. 162-163.

[184] Bearss, "Historic Structure Report...Fort Pickens," pp. 506-507.

[185] Hoag, David D., Life and Letters of Capt. David D. Hoag, compiled by his brother J.C. Hoag. (New York: 1866). Letter dated March 3, 1863, p. 52.

[186] Bearss, "Historic Structure Report...Fort Barrancas," pp. 537-54.

[187] Ibid., p. 545.

[188] R.L. Hoxie, "Report on Condition of Fortifications for Defense of Pensacola Harbor, Fiscal Year Ending June 30, 1885," a letter from Engineer Office, Montgomery, Alabama, dated August 2, 1885.

[189] Bearss, "Historic Structure Report...Endicott Battery," Vol. 1, p. 10.

[190] "Historical Report — Hurricane, September 26 and 27, 1906," Microfilm RG 392. On file at the Gulf Islands National Seashore Library.

[191] Bearss, "Historic Structure Report...Endicott Battery," Vol. 2, p. 192.

[192] Bearss, "Historical Structure Report...Endicott Battery," Vol. 1, p. 157.

[193] Robinson, American Forts, p. 97.

[194] Gjessing, "Historic Structure...Advanced Redoubt," p. 10.

[195] Dian Magie, "Fort Barrancas." Report on file at the Gulf Islands National Seashore Library, p. 4.

[196] "Fort Barrancas and Water Battery History Sheet," a guide prepared by the staff of the Gulf Islands National Seashore gives $200,000 as the cost. George F. Pearce in The U.S. Navy in Pensacola gives the figure $334,000.

[197] Magie, "Fort Barrancas," p. 4.

[198] Robinson, American Forts, p. 104.

[199] Historic American Buildings Survey No. Fla.-143. "Fort Barrancas." Unpaged.

[200] Robinson, American Forts, p. 104.

[201] Magie, "Fort Barrancas," p. 2.

[202] HABS No. Fla.-143. "Fort Barrancas." Unpaged.

[203] Robinson, American Forts, p. 104.

[204] Bearss, "Civil War Operations," p. 125.

[205] Ibid., p. 351.

[206] Langdon L. Rumph, "Letters of a Teenage Confederate," Florida Historical Quarterly 38, No. 4 (April, 1960), p. 340.

[207] Governeur Morris, The History of a Volunteer Regiment (New York: 1891), p. 48.

[208] William M. Straight, "The Pensacola Campaign Through a Nurse's Eye," Journal of the Florida Medical Association 56, No. 8 (August, 1969), p. 634.

[209] Joseph Dill Alison, "Civil War Diary," Pensacola Historical Society Quarterly 2, No. 1 (January, 1966). Entries dated May 26, 1861 and February 23, 1862.

[210] Frank H. Larned, "Letterbook and Miscellaneous Papers, 1862-1864." Manuscript collection, University of West Florida Library. Entry dated June 2, 1862.

[211] Lewis Starling, "Letters to His Father." Manuscript collection, University of West Florida Library. Letter dated July 9, 1862.

[212] William C. Hollbrook, "A Narrative of the Services of the Officers and Enlisted Men of the 7th Regiment of Vermont Volunteers," 1882. Manuscript collection, Pensacola Historical Museum, p. 117.

[213] Morris, The History of a Volunteer Regiment. Illustration.

[214] Arthur Green, "Stabilization and Restoration of an Historical Fortification," Technology and Conservation, Summer, 1977, p. 19.

[215] Ibid., p. 25.

[216] Gjessing, "Historic Structure Report...Advanced Redoubt," pp. 12-17.

[217] Frank H. Larned, "Letterbook," Entry dated May 1, 1862.

[218] Ibid., entry dated November 15, 1964.

[219] Gjessing, "Historic Structure Report...Advanced Redoubt," p. 77.

[220] Pensacola News Journal, October 30, 1976.

[221] Gjessing, "Historic Structure Report...Advanced Redoubt," p. 10.

[222] Green, "Stabilization and Restoration," p. 19.

[223] Gjessing, "Historic Structure Report...Advanced Redoubt," pp. 7-13, and HABS No. Fla.-145 used for this description.

[224] Pearce, The U.S. Navy in Pensacola, p. 44n.

[225] Staff, Gulf Islands National Seashore.

[226] Charles H. Bliss, "Pensacola's Interesting Features," Bliss Quarterly, January, 1898, p. 25.

[227] Bearss, "Historic Structure Report...Fort Barrancas," pp. 42-46.

[228] Pearce, The U.S. Navy in Pensacola, p. 25.

[229] D. Douglass Davis, Virginia Parks, and Elizabeth D. Vickers, "Fort Barrancas, 1875," Pensacola Historical Society Quarterly, Summer, 1974, p. 23. Map.

[230] Bearss, "Historic Structure Report — Fort Barrancas," pp. 255-256.

[231] Ibid., pp. 263-264.

[232] Davis, "Fort Barrancas, 1875," p. 8-10.

[233] Pensacola News-Journal, October 30, 1942.

[234] Davis, "Fort Barrancas, 1987," p. 10.

[235] Bearss, "Civil War Operations," p. 125.

[236] Pearce, The U.S. Navy in Pensacola, pp. 75-78.

[237] Bearss, "Civil War Operations," p. 352.

[238] Parks, "Pensacola in the Civil War," p. 20.

[239] Ibid., pp. 31-32.

[240] Ibid., p. 21.

[241] Pearce, The U.S. Navy in Pensacola, p. 94.

[242] Davis, "Fort Barrancas, 1875," pp. 10-13.

[243] Ibid., p. 7.

[244] Ibid., p. 14.

[245] Federal Writer's Project. Florida. Florida: A Guide to the Southernmost State. (New York: Oxford University Press, 1939), p. 448.

[246] Map, "Outlying Landing Fields," Naval Air Station, 1938. Copy on file at the Pensacola Historical Museum.

[247] Map, "Outlying Landing Fields, Naval Air Training Bases," 1947. Copy on file at the Pensacola Historical Museum.

[248] From Pirates to Pilots: A Pictorial History of Pensacola Navy, 1528 to Present. (Pensacola: Pensacola Engraving Company, 1975), pp. 49-50.

[249] Gosport, April 18, 1975, p. 1.

[250] United States Naval Aviation, 1910-1970. NAVAIR 00-80. (Washington: Government Printing Office, 1970), p. 167.

[251] O.F.G. Hogg, Artillery: Its Origin, Heydey, and Decline (London: Archon Books, 1970). Appendices I and II, pp. 264-288.

[252] D.H. Mahan, A Complete Treatise on Field Fortifications... (New York: Greenwood Press, 1968; reprint edition), p. 30.

[253] Ibid. Plate I, Figure 1, following p. 20.

[254] A.E. Forster, "U.S. Battleship Massachusetts," a

typescript from his memoirs, manuscript collection of the Pensacola Historical Museum. Mr. Forster does not give a date for these guns being in Pensacola. Mr. T.T. Wentworth, Jr., has stated it was in 1922. The Pensacola Historical Museum has photographs taken by an unknown photographer of both the cannon and the mortar, and knowledgeable persons have identified them as being a 14-inch cannon and a 12-inch mortar.

255 Staff, Gulf Islands National Seashore.

256 Ibid.

Artillerists conduct training exercises with the 12-inch gun of Battery Pensacola within the walls of Fort Pickens prior to World War I. Guns of the Pickens battery were mounted on disappearing carriages. Photo courtesy Gulf Islands National Seashore.

Index